Table of Contents

Introduction..7

Chapter 1: Everything You Need to Know About Instant Pot..9

Major Buttons..9

Preset Buttons.. 11

How to Use the Instant Pot............................. 13

Chapter 2: What Is the Ketogenic Diet?.................15

Foods to Avoid...15

Foods to Eat.. 16

Chapter 3: Instant Pot, Keto Diet Breakfast Recipes.... 18

1 - Slow-cooked Feta, Red Pepper, Kale Frittata.... 18

2 - Slow Cooked Egg & Sausage Casserole...............20

3 - Not Just Any Other Egg Casserole...................... 22

4 - Slow Cooker Egg Casserole Mexican Style.........24

5 - Overnight Slow Cooker Breakfast Casserole......26

6 - Crockpot Egg & Cauliflower Breakfast Pie.........28

7 - Breakfast Chorizo 'n Spaghettis Squash Slow Cooker.. 30

8 - Slow Cooked Egg, Spinach 'N Artichoke............32

9 - Keto-Approved Egg & Cottage Cheese Casserole34

10 - Greek Styled Slow Cooker Egg Casserole......... 36

11 - Tomatoes, Cheese, and Herb Omelet................ 38

12 - Instant Pot Low-Carb Oatmeal........................... 40

13 - Coconut and Psyllium Porridge....................... 41

14 - Breakfast Cajun-Cauliflower Hash................... 42

15 - Moroccan Styled Breakfast Eggs......................44

Chapter 4 – Instant Pot, Keto Diet Appetizer Recipes. 46

16 - Garlic-Flavored Shrimp.......................................46

17 - Keto Appetizing Scallop Dish............................ 48

18 - Roasted Garlic Cauliflower Mash..................... 50

19 - Goat Cheese and Prosciutto Wrapped Asparagus.. 52

20 – Spinach, Roasted Garlic, and Bacon Dip........ 54

21 – Crab, Bacon, And Poblano Spicy Dip.............. 56

22 - Stuffed Mushrooms with Curried Shrimp....... 58

23 – Deviled Eggs in Instant Pot............................. 60

24 – Pan-Fried Portobello Mushrooms Mediterranean Style... 62

25 – Instant Pot Appetizing Meatballs.................... 64

Chapter 5 – Instant Pot, Keto Diet Poultry Recipes......66

26 – Herbed Butter Over Chicken Breast............... 66

27 – Cream Cheese Sauce Over Turkey....................68

28 – Chicken Curry Malaysian Style........................ 70

29 – Chicken casserole with Olives, Cheese, and Pesto..72

30 – Chicken Casserole with Tomatoes, Cauliflower, and Pesto... 74

31 – Chicken Stew Belize Style...........................76

32 – Chicken Adobo Filipino Style.....................78

33 – Lettuce Turkey Wrap..................................80

34 – Keto-Approved Turkey Burger....................82

35 – Chili with Shredded Chicken......................84

Chapter 6 – Instant Pot, Keto Diet Meat Recipes......... 86

36 – Mushroom Bacon Cheeseburger Lettuce Wraps..86

37 – Red Pesto Chops.......................................88

38 – Herbed and Buttered Lamb Chops.................90

39 – Keto Approved Beef Stroganoff.....................92

40 – Blue Cheese Sauce Pork Chops....................94

41 – Béarnaise Sauce over Steak....................... 96

42 – Patties with Tomato Sauce and Fried Cabbage98

43 – Cabbage Stir-Fry Indian Style..................... 100

44 – Moroccan Beef Slow Cooked.......................102

45 – Tex-Mex Casserole Keto Style......................104

46 – Pressure cooked lamb shanks......................106

47 – Goat Curry..108

48 – Slow Cooked Lamb the Keto Way..................110

49 – Mutton Curry Keto.................................... 112

50 – Protein Noodle Lasagna............................ 114

Chapter 7 – Instant Pot, Keto Diet Soup Recipes........116

51 – Easy Lobster Bisque in Instant Pot................ 116

52 – Coconut-Mussels Thai Style.........................119 ←

53 – Leek and Broccoli Creamy Soup....................121

54 – Turkey Asian Soup with Cilantro Butter.......123

55 – Mushroom Cream Soup................................125

56 – Low Carb Cabbage Roll Soup.......................127

57 – Ground beef and peppers in Goulash Soup.. 129

58 – Chicken Green Chili....................................131 ←

59 – Keto Style Zuppa Toscana........................... 133

60 – Instant Pot Seafood Medley Stew................. 135

Chapter 8 – Instant Pot, Keto Diet Seafood Recipes.. 137

61 – Poached and Herbed Salmon......................... 137

62 – Slow-Cooked Garlic-Herbed Mussels............139

63 – Instant Pot Poached Lemon & Herb Cod......141

64 – Slow-Cooked Marinara Squid.......................143

65 – Caper-Relish Topped Poached Salmon.........144

66 – Arugula Tapenade Over Cod.........................146

67 – Oriental Style Fish Curry............................ 148

68 – Braised Sea Bass in Instant Pot....................150

69 – Shrimp Scampi on Spaghetti Squash........... 152

70 – Easy Steamed Golden Pomfret..................... 154

Chapter 9 - Instant Pot, Keto Diet Vegetable Recipes 156

71 – Nasi Goreng Keto Approved............................ 156

72 – Cabbage Asian Stir-Fry..................................... 158

73 – Brussel Sprouts with Bacon..........................160

74 – Red Coconut Curry Vegetarian...................... 162

75 – Stir Fry Tempeh, Spinach, Broccoli and Olives164

Chapter 10 –Instant Pot, Keto Vegan-Friendly Recipes166

76 – Keto Fries with Peppers and Caramelized Cauliflower... 166

77 – Cauliflower Rice..168

78 – Keto-Approved Steamed Artichoke.............. 169

79 – Vegetarian Soy Curls with Butter Chicken....171

80 – Brussels Sprouts, Spinach and Hummus..... 173

Chapter 10 – Instant Pot, Keto Dessert Recipes..........175

81 – Cream and Berries Cake with Whipped Brown Sugar.. 175

82 – Chocolate Salty Treat...................................... 177

83 – Chocolate Fudge..179

84 – Macadamia Nut Brownies.............................. 181

85 – Mocha Pudding Cake..................................... 183

Introduction

The ketogenic diet is one of the most popular weight loss diets that promise results. It encourages dieters to reduce their carbohydrate intake to promote the body to use ketones and fats as a source of energy. Under this circumstance, the body is able to burn off fats at a faster rate.

Preparing your own meals is essential for the keto diet. However, most dieters do not know how to prepare healthy yet delicious keto-friendly meals. This is where the Instant Pot comes into the picture.

Since most ketogenic-friendly foods are mostly meat, they require you to slave in the kitchen. With Instant Pot, you can place the ingredients in the pot and it will be ready after a few minutes—not too much stirring involved. The healthy dishes that you can prepare with an Instant Pot will always satisfy your hunger so that you do not get tempted to grab sugary snacks.

Making ketogenic-friendly meals with your Instant Pot is a unique idea so if you are looking for good references, then we got you covered. This eBook is your best resource for the ketogenic diet and Instant Pot recipes combined. Everything you need about this topic is discussed in this eBook. Happy reading!

Chapter 1: Everything You Need to Know About Instant Pot

The Instant Pot is a third-generation digital pressure cooker that allows you to cook different types of foods with just a press of a button. Unlike conventional pressure cookers, the Instant Pot can also function as a slow cooker, rice cooker, yogurt maker, steamer, and warming pot. Although the functions of the Instant Pot can be overwhelming, using it is not difficult at all. Thus, this chapter will discuss about what you need to know about Instant Pot.

Major Buttons

The Instant Pot comes with major buttons that are located at the base of the control panel. These buttons allow you to make adjustments on the settings on your Instant Pot so you can turn your Instant Pot into a yogurt-maker, slow cooker, and many others. Below are the major buttons of the Instant Pot.

- +/-: This particular button allows you to make changes on the cooking time. So, if you need to cook food for longer, press the "+" button and "-" if you want your food to cook at a shorter time.

- **Adjust:** This button allows you to change the default temperature to something that you want to use. Use the adjust button together with the preset cooking buttons that will be explained later.

- **Slow cook:** This button lets your convert your Instant Pot into a crockpot. You can cook your food slowly so that it is ready by the time you get back.

- **Sauté:** You can sauté food with the Instant Pot so that you can brown or simmer food while the lid is open. Use the adjust button to change the temperature setting of the sauté mode.

- **Yogurt:** What makes the Instant Pot great is that you can make your own yogurt and other fermented foods with this machine.

- **Timer:** The timer button allows you to set how long you want to cook your food. Once the timer sets off, the Instant Pot will immediately turn off. The delayed timer, in particular, allows you to cook food at a later specified time.

- **Manual:** This button lets you set the cooking time that you want to cook your food. With this button, you have full control on how you will cook your food. Press the + or - button to adjust the cooking time.

- **Pressure:** This button allows you to change the pressure cooking method from high to low and vice versa.

- **Keep Warm/Cancel:** It allows you to turn off the Instant Pot or function as a warmer.

Preset Buttons

The preset buttons on the Instant Pot are perfect for people who are new to cooking different types of food. They come with preset time, temperature, and pressure settings so that the food is cooked properly and evenly. These buttons remove the guesswork in your cooking. Below are the different types of preset buttons that are available on the Instant Pot.

- **Meat/Stew:** This button will cook pork, beef, lamb, and other game meats at high pressure for 35 minutes.

- **Poultry:** Chicken, turkey, and other types of game bird meat can be cooked on high for 15 minutes under this preset button. Do not use a longer cooking time because the texture of the meat might get too rubbery.

- **Bean/Chili:** Cook different types of bean dishes with this preset button. It cooks dry beans for 30 minutes at high pressure. Soaked beans can be cooked at lower cooking time.

- **Porridge/Congee:** Make soft congee and porridge with this preset button. It allows you to cook congee at high pressure for 20 minutes.

- **Soup:** Make different soups with this button. You can cook hearty soups and stews for 40 minutes under high pressure.

- **Multigrain:** Cook quinoa, wheat, barley and other grains except rice with this preset button for 40 minutes at high pressure.

- **Rice:** Cook different types of rice with this button. This preset button cannot be adjusted so if you are going to cook hardier types of rice grains like brown or black rice, choose the Manual button.

- **Steam:** Put the steamer rack inside and you can cook amazing steamed dishes with this button.

But aside from that, you can also use this button to cook fish and vegetables.

If you are following the ketogenic diet, you are prohibited from consuming grains and sugar so there are some preset buttons that you don't need such as the rice, multigrain, and porridge.

How to Use the Instant Pot

Using the Instant Pot is not difficult at all! Contrary to what most people think, it works in a dump-and-forget system so you only need to put all ingredients in the pot, press the desired cooking button and forget about it until it is finished cooking. But for safety purposes, below are tips on how to use the Instant Pot.

- **Place enough liquid when cooking:** Do not a little amount of liquid in the Instant Pot. As a general rule, the Instant Pot needs a minimum of 1 ½ cups of liquid that may come from water, seasonings, and stock to maintain a good cooking pressure.

- **Don't overfill the pot with liquid:** While too little liquid does not produce enough pressure, too much of it will result from liquid flowing out from the steam vent. So, whether you are cooking

13

soup, stew, rice, or congee, make sure that the liquid does not go beyond the *max line* as indicated in the inner pot.

- **Always tilt the lid when opening:** The seam inside the Instant Pot is scalding so make sure that you tilt the lid when opening so that you don't get steam on your face.

- **Never use force to open the lid:** If the lid is not opening, do not use force to open it. It does not mean that the lid is stuck. It simply indicates that the pressure inside the pot has not reduced. Either wait for the pressure to get stable or do quick pressure release.

- **Clean the pot after use:** Make it a habit to clean the Instant Pot after every use. Pay extra attention to the inner pot, lid, sealing gaskets, and O-rings. Use water to clean these parts. Regarding the external body of the pot, wipe it with damp cloth. Never expose the electrical parts with water. When cleaning your pot, take note if there are any damages that need to be addressed and fixed.

Chapter 2: What Is the Ketogenic Diet?

The premise about the ketogenic diet is to consume foods that are low in carbohydrates so that the body is pushed to the state of ketosis wherein it burns fat instead of carbohydrates as a source of fuel. Similar with other low-carb diets such as the Atkins Diet, the only difference with this particular diet is that it encourages dieters to consume adequate amounts of proteins. Thus, with this particular diet, the insulin levels become stable and your body's fat metabolism is also increased.

Foods to Avoid

- **Grains:** Grains like wheat, cereal, rice, corn, and many others should be avoided as they contain high amounts of carbohydrates that are converted into glucose.

- **Sugar:** Sugar either sourced from refined or natural products should be avoided. These include white sugar, fruits, dates, honey, maple syrup, and coconut sugar to name a few.

- **Fruits:** Fruits contain high amounts of fructose, which is a form of simple sugar. Avoid eating starchy fruits like bananas and apples. You can eat berries but in moderation.

- **Root crops:** Root crops like jicama, potatoes, sweet potatoes, yam, taro should be avoided because they contain complex carbohydrates.

Foods to Eat

- **Vegetables:** You can eat vegetables that grow above the ground as they do not contain high amounts of starches. These include broccoli, cauliflower, cabbages, and other leafy greens.

- **Meats:** Lean meats from lamb, fish, pork, beef, and poultry should be eaten at appropriate amounts.

- **High fat dairy products:** Products like butter, hard cheese, full fat cream, and milk are high in fat thus good for the ketogenic diet.

- **Nuts and seeds:** Nuts like pistachios, macadamias, sunflower seeds, and walnuts contain good sources of healthy fats to boost the state of ketosis in your body.

- **Low-carb sweeteners:** People on a ketogenic diet can still eat sweet foods as long as they are flavored with low-carb sweeteners like erythritol and stevia as they do not impact the blood sugar levels.

- **Fats:** Healthy fats found in coconut oil, butter, avocado and other sources for saturated fats is also good for the ketogenic diet.

- **Berries:** You can still eat fruits under this diet as long as they are berries as they have low glycemic index. They are also good sources of antioxidants and nutrients.

Chapter 3: Instant Pot, Keto Diet Breakfast Recipes

1 - Slow-cooked Feta, Red Pepper, Kale Frittata

Serves: 6
Cooking Time: 2 hours and 30 minutes
Preparation Time: 20 minutes

Ingredients:
- ½ teaspoon salt
- ½ teaspoon pepper
- 8 eggs, well beaten
- 4-ounce crumbled Feta
- ¼ cup sliced green onion
- 6-ounce roasted red pepper, drained and chopped
- Cooking spray
- 5-ounce baby kale
- 2 teaspoons olive oil

Instructions:
1) Wash kale and dry with a paper towel or use a spin dryer.
2) On instant pot, press sauté button.
3) Add oil to inner pot.

4) Sauté kale around 2 minutes or until soft and flat.
5) Evenly spread kale on bottom of pot.
6) Add and evenly spread feta, green onions, and red pepper.
7) In bowl of beaten eggs, whisk in salt and pepper.
8) Pour beaten eggs into Crockpot.
9) Cover, press slow cook button, press pressure and choose HIGH.
10) Cook for 2 ½-hours.

Nutrition information: Calories per serving: 107; Carbohydrates: 5.4g; Protein: 8.86g; Fat: 5.89g; Sugar: 3.17g; Sodium: 517mg; Fiber: 1.3g

2 - Slow Cooked Egg & Sausage Casserole

Serves: 6
Cooking Time: 5 hours
Preparation Time: 20 minutes

Ingredients:
- ¼ teaspoon pepper
- ½ teaspoon salt
- 2 cloves garlic, minced
- ¾ cup whipping cream
- 10 eggs
- 1 cup shredded Cheddar cheese, divided
- 1 12-ounce package Jones Dairy Farm Little Links, cooked and sliced
- 1 medium head broccoli, chopped

Instructions:
1) Grease the sides and bottom of the inner pot with a cooking spray.
2) Using one-half of the broccoli, sausage, and cheese, evenly spread in Instant Pot with sausage first, followed by broccoli, and lastly the cheese.
3) Repeat the same process with the remaining broccoli, sausage, and cheese.

4) Whisk well pepper, salt, garlic, whipping cream, and eggs in a large bowl.
5) Pour egg mixture into Instant Pot.
6) Cover, press slow cook button, press pressure button and select LOW.
7) Cook for 5 hours or until the casserole is set and edges are browned.

Nutrition information: Calories per serving: 378; Carbohydrates: 2.81g; Protein: 27.16g; Fat: 28.09g; Sugar: 1.06g; Sodium: mg; Fiber: 0.2g

3 - Not Just Any Other Egg Casserole

Serves: 6
Cooking Time: 2 hours and 35 minutes
Preparation Time: 20 minutes

Ingredients:
- 1 8-ounce package of sharp Cheddar Fine Cut cheese
- ½ teaspoon salt, divided
- 6 eggs
- 1 leek, cleaned and cut into ¼-inch half-moon slices
- 12 fully cooked sausage links, cut into ¼-inch circles
- 5-ounce cremini mushrooms, finely diced
- 10-ounce cauliflower, chopped into bite-sized florets

Instructions:
1) With cooking spray grease the sides and bottom of your Instant Pot.
2) In a large and microwave safe bowl, place cauliflower in bowl. Cover with water and add ¼ teaspoon salt. Microwave for 8 minutes on high.
3) Drain cauliflower and transfer to Instant Pot.
4) Then evenly spread sausage and mushrooms on top of cauliflower.
5) In a large bowl, whisk well the eggs and remaining salt. Stir in half of the cheese and then the leeks.
6) Pour egg mixture in Instant Pot.

7) Cover Instant Pot, press slow cook button, and then press pressure button and select HIGH.
8) Cook the casserole until eggs puff up, around 2 ½-hours.
9) Once done cooking, sprinkle remaining cheese on top of casserole. Cover and let it melt for 5 minutes.
10) Serve and enjoy.

Nutrition information: Calories per serving: 426; Carbohydrates: 6.54g; Protein: 22.68g; Fat: 34.67g; Sugar: 2.42g; Sodium: 934mg; Fiber: 1.4g

4 - Slow Cooker Egg Casserole Mexican Style

Serves: 10
Cooking Time: 5 hours
Preparation Time: 15 minutes

Ingredients:

- 1 cup pepper jack
- 1 cup milk
- 10 eggs
- 1 cup salsa
- ¼ teaspoon pepper
- ¼ teaspoon salt
- 1 teaspoon chili powder
- 1 teaspoon cumin
- ½ teaspoon coriander
- ½ teaspoon garlic powder
- 12-ounces Jones Dairy Farm Pork Sausage Roll

Instructions:

1) On Instant Pot, press sauté button and cook pork sausage until cooked and no longer pink.
2) Once cooked, stir in chili powder, cumin, coriander, and garlic powder and sauté for a minute.
3) Pour in salsa, mix well, and press warming button.
4) Meanwhile, in a large bowl whisk well eggs, milk, pepper, and salt.

5) Pour egg mixture into Instant Pot and mix well.
6) Add cheese, whisk well.
7) Cover, press slow cook button, press pressure button and select LOW.
8) Cook for 5 hours.

Nutrition information: Calories per serving: 320; Carbohydrates: 5.2g; Protein: 17.9g; Fat: 24.1g; Sugar: 1.6g; Sodium: 749mg; Fiber: 0.8g

5 - Overnight Slow Cooker Breakfast Casserole

Serves: 8
Cooking Time: 8 hours and 30 minutes
Preparation Time: 30 minutes

Ingredients:
- 1/8 teaspoon pepper
- ½ teaspoon salt
- 1 cup milk
- 12 eggs
- 1 ½ cups shredded Cheddar cheese
- ¼ cup chopped fresh cilantro
- 1 4-ounce can of diced mild green chilies
- 1 sweet red bell pepper, chopped
- 1 cup chopped green onions
- 2 12-ounce packages Johnsonville Original Breakfast Sausage

Instructions:
1) Grease Instant Pot with cooking spray.
2) Sauté breakfast sausage in Instant Pot according to package instructions and slice into ¼-inch thick circles.
3) Mix cilantro, chilies, red pepper, and green onions in a bowl.

4) Whisk eggs pepper, salt, and milk in another bowl.
5) Spread ½ of the sliced sausages on the bottom of pot, followed by ½ of the green onion mixture, and lastly ½ of the cheese. Repeat the same layering process to the remaining sausages, green onion mixture, and cheese.
6) Whisk eggs one last time and evenly pour on top of the layered mixture.
7) Cover, press slow cook button, and set Instant Pot pressure on low.
8) Cook for 6 hours or until instant read thermometer shows 160°F.

Nutrition information: Calories per serving: 439; Carbohydrates: 12.3g; Protein: 31.25g; Fat: 31.16g; Sugar: 2.64g; Sodium: 1247mg; Fiber: 2.7g

6 - Crockpot Egg & Cauliflower Breakfast Pie

Serves: 6
Cooking Time: 8 hours
Preparation Time: 25 minutes

Ingredients:
- Pepper and salt to taste
- 2 teaspoons dried basil
- 1 tablespoon garlic powder
- 1 yellow onion, diced
- 1-pound US Wellness Meat pork sausage, broken up
- 2 cups cauliflower, chopped finely
- 8 eggs, whisked

Instructions:
1) Ready your Instant Pot by greasing the sides and the bottom with cooking spray.
2) Evenly spread the pork sausage on bottom of pot.
3) Spread chopped onions evenly on top of sausage.
4) Then top with the finely chopped cauliflower.
5) In a bowl, whisk eggs. Season with pepper and salt generously. Whisk in garlic powder.
6) Pour into Instant Pot.
7) Cover, press slow cook button, set pressure on low setting.

8) Cook for 8 hours.

Nutrition information: Calories per serving: 353; Carbohydrates: 6.51g; Protein: 22.62g; Fat: 26.33g; Sugar: 2.55g; Sodium: 711mg; Fiber: 1.4g

7 - Breakfast Chorizo 'n Spaghettis Squash Slow Cooker

Serves: 4
Cooking Time: 4 hours
Preparation Time: 40 minutes

Ingredients:
- ¼ cup chopped cilantro for garnish
- 4 large eggs
- ½ cup salsa Verde
- ½ cup cheddar cheese, shredded
- 2 cups cooked spaghetti squash
- ¼ cup Mexican Chorizo
- 1 tablespoon olive oil

Instructions:
1) Begin by cooking your spaghetti squash. To do this, pierce squash all over with fork. Place on a microwave safe plate and microwave for 20 minutes.
2) Once squash is done cooking, remove from microwave and let it cool for at least 5 minutes. Cut squash in half, scoop and discard the seeds. Then remove 2 cups of stringy flesh and set aside.
3) Add oil to Instant Pot and press sauté button.
4) Sauté Mexican chorizo for 5 minutes or until no longer pink.

5) Then press the warm button.
6) In a large bowl, whisk eggs. Mix in salsa verde and cheese.
7) Pour egg mixture into Instant Pot and mix well with the chorizo.
8) Cover, press slow cook button, and set pressure on medium.
9) Cook for 4 hours.
10) To serve, sprinkle cilantro leaves on top of casserole.

Nutrition information: Calories per serving: 236; Carbohydrates: 7.99g; Protein: 10.27g; Fat: 18.28g; Sugar: 3.16g; Sodium: 449mg; Fiber: 1.7g

8 - Slow Cooked Egg, Spinach 'N Artichoke

Serves: 12
Cooking Time: 8 hours
Preparation Time: 15 minutes

Ingredients:
- ½ teaspoon crushed red pepper
- ½ teaspoon dried thyme
- 1 teaspoon salt
- 1 garlic clove, minced
- ¼ cup shaved onion
- ½ cup ricotta cheese
- 1 cup shredded white cheddar
- 10-ounce box frozen chopped spinach, thawed, and drained well
- 14-ounce can artichoke hearts, drained
- ¼ cup milk
- 16 large eggs

Instructions:
1) In a large bowl, whisk well eggs. Stir in milk and salt.
2) With paper towel, squeeze spinach leaves to wring out excess water. Add into bowl of eggs.
3) Chop artichoke into small pieces and separate the leaves. Add into bowl of eggs and mix well.

4) Add red pepper, dried thyme, garlic clove, onions, and white cheddar cheese into bowl of eggs. Mix well.
5) Ready Instant Pot by greasing sides and bottom with cooking spray.
6) Pour in egg mixture.
7) Evenly add dollops of ricotta cheese on top of the egg mixture.
8) Cover, press slow cook button, and choose the low pressure.
9) Cook for 8 hours or until sides are lightly browned and the eggs have set.

Nutrition information: Calories per serving: 180; Carbohydrates: 6.99g; Protein: 13.14g; Fat: 11.17g; Sugar: 1.68g; Sodium: 383mg; Fiber: 3.3g

9 - Keto-Approved Egg & Cottage Cheese Casserole

Serves: 4
Cooking Time: minutes
Preparation Time: 10 minutes

Ingredients:
- 4-ounce Feta
- 1/8 teaspoon nutmeg
- ½ teaspoon dill weed, dry
- 6 large egg whites
- 1 16-ounce tub of whipped cottage cheese
- 16-ounce bag of frozen spinach, thawed and drained well
- 1 large clove of garlic, minced
- ½ medium sweet onion, diced

Instructions:
1) In large bowl, whisk egg whites.
2) Stir in feta, nutmeg, dill weed, and garlic.
3) Whisk in cottage cheese until thoroughly mixed.
4) With a paper towel, squeeze out excess moisture from the drained spinach. Add to bowl of eggs and mix well.
5) With a cooking spray, grease all sides and bottom of Instant Pot.

6) Evenly spread diced onion on bottom of pot.
7) Pour in egg mixture.
8) Cover and cook on low setting for 4 hours.

Nutrition information: Calories per serving: 318; Carbohydrates: 14.11g; Protein: 25.12g; Fat: 17.73g; Sugar: 7.67g; Sodium: 756mg; Fiber: 3.9g

10 - Greek Styled Slow Cooker Egg Casserole

Serves: 6
Cooking Time: 5 hours
Preparation Time: 15 minutes

Ingredients:
- ½ cup feta cheese
- 2 cups spinach
- 1 cup baby Bella mushrooms (sliced)
- ½ cup sun dried tomatoes
- 1 teaspoon garlic, minced
- 1 tablespoon red onion, chopped
- 1 teaspoon black pepper
- ½ teaspoon salt
- ½ cup milk
- 12 eggs, whisked

Instructions:
1) In a large bowl, whisk eggs.
2) Season with pepper and salt.
3) Mix in milk, garlic, and red onion.
4) Mix thoroughly in spinach, mushrooms, and sun-dried tomatoes.
5) With cooking spray, grease sides and bottom of Instant Pot.

6) Pour the egg mixture in Instant Pot.
7) Evenly sprinkle feta cheese on top of egg mixture.
8) Cover, press slow cook button, press pressure button, and select low pressure.
9) Cook on low for 5 hours or until eggs are set and sides are lightly browned.

Nutrition information: Calories per serving: 191; Carbohydrates: 6.13g; Protein: 14.98g; Fat: 11.94g; Sugar: 3.99g; Sodium: 462mg; Fiber: 1.1g

11 - Tomatoes, Cheese, and Herb Omelet

Serves: 2
Cooking Time: 15 minutes
Preparation Time: 5 minutes

Ingredients:
- Pepper and salt to taste
- 1/3-pounds fresh mozzarella cheese
- 1 tablespoon fresh basil or dried basil
- 3.5-ounce cherry tomatoes, halved
- 6 eggs
- 2 tablespoons olive oil

Instructions:
1) In a bowl, whisk eggs.
2) Season with pepper and salt.
3) Stir in basil and whisk well.
4) On Instant Pot, press sauté button.
5) Heat oil and ensure to coat bottom and sides of pot with oil.
6) Add tomatoes and sauté for 3 minutes.
7) Pour egg mixture.
8) Continue sautéing until slightly set and then add the cheese.
9) Continue cooking for 3 minutes.

10) Press keep warm button, cover and let it continue to set for another 5 minutes.

Nutrition information: Calories per serving: 578; Carbohydrates: 10.81g; Protein: 33.32g; Fat: 44.61g; Sugar: 7.61g; Sodium: 719mg; Fiber: 1.1g

12 - Instant Pot Low-Carb Oatmeal

Serves: 1
Cooking Time: 10 minutes
Preparation Time: 3 minutes

Ingredients:
- A pinch of salt
- 1 tablespoon sunflower seeds
- 1 tablespoon chia seeds
- 1 tablespoon flax seeds, whole
- 1 cup coconut milk

Instructions:
1) In Instant Pot, mix all ingredients.
2) Press sauté button and bring to a simmer while mixing every now and then.
3) Once mixture starts to simmer, stir frequently.
4) Continue to boil until desired consistency is achieved.

Nutrition information: Calories per serving: 689; Carbohydrates: 20.16g; Protein: 10.09g; Fat: 68.4g; Sugar: 8.27g; Sodium: 194mg; Fiber: 9.5g

13 - Coconut and Psyllium Porridge

Serves: 1
Cooking Time: 10 minutes
Preparation Time: 5 minutes

Ingredients:
- A pinch of salt
- 4 tablespoons coconut cream
- 1 pinch ground psyllium husk
- 1 tablespoon coconut flour
- 1 egg
- 1-ounce butter

Instructions:
1) Press sauté button on Instant Pot.
2) Add all ingredients, mix well, and bring to a simmer.
3) Stir every now and then.
4) Once mixture is simmering, stir mixture constantly.
5) Continue cooking until desired thickness is reached.

Nutrition information: Calories per serving: 364; Carbohydrates: 15.54g; Protein: 8.1g; Fat: 30.45g; Sugar: 2.13g; Sodium: 452mg; Fiber: 0.7g

14 - Breakfast Cajun-Cauliflower Hash

Serves: 2
Cooking Time: 15 minutes
Preparation Time: 10 minutes

Ingredients:
- ½ green bell pepper, chopped into ¼-inch pieces
- 8-ounce shaved red pastrami, chopped into 1-inch slices
- 1 teaspoon Cajun seasoning
- 1-pound bag frozen cauliflower, chopped roughly
- 2 tablespoons minced garlic
- ½ onion, chopped into ¼-inch pieces
- 2 tablespoons olive oil

Instructions:
1) In a blender or food processor, add roughly chopped cauliflower and burr until you have even rice-like flakes. Set aside.
2) On Instant Pot, press sauté button.
3) And heat oil.
4) Stir in garlic and cook until lightly browned, around 2 minutes.
5) Stir in onions and Cajun seasoning. Sauté for a minute.

6) Add burred cauliflower and sauté for 5 minutes or until lightly browned.
7) Stir in green pepper and pastrami.
8) Continue sautéing for another 5 minutes.

Nutrition information: Calories per serving: 231; Carbohydrates: 23.46g; Protein: 6.71g; Fat: 14.56g; Sugar: 9.96g; Sodium: 173mg; Fiber: 7.3g

15 - Moroccan Styled Breakfast Eggs

Serves: 2
Cooking Time: 15 minutes
Preparation Time: 5 minutes

Ingredients:
- ½ teaspoon sea salt
- ¼ teaspoon ground cayenne
- ¼ teaspoon ground cumin
- 4 eggs
- ½ cup fresh parsley, chopped
- ½ cup fresh cilantro, chopped
- 1 teaspoon fresh thyme leaves
- 2 garlic cloves, peeled and chopped finely
- 1 tablespoon coconut oil
- 2 tablespoons butter

Instructions:
1) On Instant Pot, press sauté function.
2) Add butter and coconut oil and heat for 2 minutes or until melted and hot.
3) Stir in garlic and sauté for 3 minutes or until lightly browned.
4) Add thyme and cook for a minute.
5) Stir in parsley and cilantro and cook until it starts to crisp, around 3 minutes.

6) Then break the eggs into the pan, being careful not to break the yolks.
7) Cover Instant Pot while on sauté function and cook for 3 minutes if you want the yolk to be runny. If you want the yolks to be cooked more, cook longer, around 4 to 6 minutes

Nutrition information: Calories per serving: 311; Carbohydrates: 3.08g; Protein: 12.8g; Fat: 27.5g; Sugar: 0.56g; Sodium: 809mg; Fiber: 1g

Chapter 4 – Instant Pot, Keto Diet Appetizer Recipes

16 - Garlic-Flavored Shrimp

Serves: 6
Cooking Time: 10 minutes
Preparation Time: 5 minutes

Ingredients:
- 1 tablespoon minced flat-leaf parsley, for garnish
- 2-pounds extra-large raw shrimp, peeled and deveined
- ¼ teaspoon crushed red pepper flakes
- ¼ teaspoon freshly ground black pepper
- 1 teaspoon kosher salt
- 1 teaspoon smoked Spanish paprika
- 6 cloves garlic, sliced thinly
- ¾ cup extra-virgin olive oil

Instructions:
1) Press sauté function.
2) Heat oil.
3) Sauté garlic until lightly browned, around 2 minutes.
4) Stir in crushed red pepper flakes, black pepper, salt, and paprika.

5) Cook for a minute or until fragrant.
6) Then stir in shrimps and continue cooking until pink, around 5 minutes.

Nutrition information: Calories per serving: 280; Carbohydrates: 2.7g; Protein: 30.7g; Fat: 16g; Sugar: 0g; Sodium: 386.7mg; Fiber: 0g

17 - Keto Appetizing Scallop Dish

Serves: 3
Cooking Time: 10 minutes
Preparation Time: 5 minutes

Ingredients:
- Pepper and salt to taste
- 1-pound bay scallops
- 2 cloves garlic, halved
- 2 thyme sprigs or to taste
- 1 lemon, sliced
- 3 tablespoons butter
- 1 teaspoon olive oil

Instructions:
1) Press sauté button of Instant Pot.
2) Heat oil.
3) Stir in garlic and sauté until lightly browned, around 2 minutes.
4) Add thyme, lemon, and butter. Cook for a minute or until butter is fully melted.
5) Add scallops and cook for 3 minutes per side.
6) Season with pepper and salt to taste and mix well.
7) To serve, sprinkle with parsley (optional).

Nutrition information: Calories per serving: 284; Carbohydrates: 11.76g; Protein: 31.75g; Fat: 12.89g; Sugar: 1.2g; Sodium: 1102mg; Fiber: 0.5g

18 - Roasted Garlic Cauliflower Mash

Serves: 4
Cooking Time: 15 minutes
Preparation Time: 10 minutes

Ingredients:
- Pepper to taste
- 4-ounce butter
- 1-pound cauliflower
- ½ teaspoon salt
- 1 whole garlic, smashed and chopped finely
- 1 tablespoon olive oil

Instructions:
1) Chop cauliflower roughly and place in blender or food processor. Process until rice-like in appearance but not mushy. If needed, squeeze out excess water and set aside.
2) In Instant Pot, heat oil.
3) Sauté garlic until lightly browned, around two minutes.
4) Add butter and once melted, stir in cauliflower rice.
5) Season with salt and pepper.
6) Sauté cauliflower for 10 minutes or until tender and soft and easy to mash.

7) Remove from pot and mash with fork, serve, and enjoy.

Nutrition information: Calories per serving: 269; Carbohydrates: 6.73g; Protein: 2.65g; Fat: 27.05g; Sugar: 2.76g; Sodium: 508mg; Fiber: 2.4g

19 - Goat Cheese and Prosciutto Wrapped Asparagus

Serves: 6
Cooking Time: 10 minutes
Preparation Time: 15 minutes

Ingredients:
- 2 tablespoons olive oil
- ¼ teaspoon ground black pepper
- 5-ounce goat cheese
- 6 slices prosciutto
- 12 pieces of green asparagus

Instructions:
1) Slice the cheese into 6 slices and then divide into two each slice.
2) Wash and trim asparagus.
3) Slice ham into two lengthwise.
4) Wrap one slice of ham around two pieces of cheese and one asparagus. Repeat this process until all asparagus and cheese are wrapped.
5) On Instant Pot, arrange asparagus evenly in one layer.
6) Drizzle olive oil on asparagus and sprinkle pepper.
7) Press the sauté function and sauté 3 minutes per side.

Nutrition information: Calories per serving: 390; Carbohydrates: 5.18g; Protein: 43.15g; Fat: 22.5g; Sugar: 4.46g; Sodium: 2392mg; Fiber: 0.7g

20 – Spinach, Roasted Garlic, and Bacon Dip

Serves: 6
Cooking Time: 30 minutes
Preparation Time: 10 minutes

Ingredients:
- Pepper and salt to taste
- 8-ounces cream cheese, softened
- ½ cup sour cream
- 5-ounces fresh spinach
- 2.5-ounces parmesan cheese, grated
- 1 ½ tablespoons fresh parsley, chopped
- 1 tablespoon roasted garlic
- 1 tablespoon lemon juice
- 6 slices bacon

Instructions:
1) On Instant Pot, press sauté function and cook bacon until crisped, around 8 minutes.
2) Transfer crisped bacon to a plate. Crumble bacon and set aside.
3) In bacon grease, sauté spinach until wilted, around three minutes.

4) Add cream cheese, sour cream, parmesan cheese, parsley, ½ of the crumbled bacon, and lemon juice. Mix well.
5) Cover, press porridge button, and adjust cooking time to 15 minutes.
6) Once cooked, transfer to a serving bowl and sprinkle remaining bacon on top.
7) Serve with keto-approved chips, veggies, or stick bread.

Nutrition information: Calories per serving: 302; Carbohydrates: 6.12g; Protein: 10.78g; Fat: 26.46g; Sugar: 1.78g; Sodium: 536mg; Fiber: 0.6g

21 – Crab, Bacon, And Poblano Spicy Dip

Serves: 10
Cooking Time: 25 minutes
Preparation Time: 10 minutes

Ingredients:
- Pepper to taste
- 1 cup shaved Parmesan cheese, divided
- 2 tablespoon lemon juice
- 4 large garlic cloves, minced
- 4 green onion, minced
- 2 poblano peppers, diced
- ½ cup mayonnaise
- ½ cup sour cream
- 8-ounce cream cheese, softened
- 8 strips thick cut bacon, sliced into lardons
- 12-ounce crab meat

Instructions:
1) In blender or food processor, process mayo, sour cream, and cream cheese until smooth.
2) Add ½ cup of parmesan, lemon juice, garlic, poblano, and ½ of green onion. Process until roughly chopped and roughly incorporated—not smooth and creamy.

3) On Instant Pot, press sauté button and crisp fry bacon, around 8 minutes.
4) Crumble bacon and set aside.
5) Press warm on Instant Pot.
6) Transfer mixture from food processor into Instant pot.
7) Add the crab meat and crumbled bacon into Instant Pot and fold gently until lightly mixed.
8) Cover, press porridge function, and adjust cooking time to 15 minutes.
9) Transfer to a serving bowl, garnish with remaining green onions, and enjoy.

Nutrition information: Calories per serving: 250; Carbohydrates: 5.48g; Protein: 11.87g; Fat: 20.36g; Sugar: 1.86g; Sodium: 611mg; Fiber: 0.4g

22 - Stuffed Mushrooms with Curried Shrimp

Serves: 20
Cooking Time: 20 minutes
Preparation Time: 10 minutes

Ingredients:
- 20-pcs white mushrooms
- 1 cup cooked shrimp
- ½ cup shredded Mexican blend cheese
- 4-ounce low fat cream cheese, softened
- ¼ cup sour cream
- ¼ cup mayo
- 1 teaspoon curry powder
- 1 teaspoon salt
- 1 teaspoon garlic powder
- ½ small onion, finely chopped
- 1 tablespoon oil

Instructions:
1) Roughly chop cooked shrimps and set aside.
2) Mix well cream cheese, shredded cheese, sour cream, mayo, garlic powder, onion, curry, and seasoned salt.
3) Stir in chopped shrimps.
4) Remove the stems from the mushrooms and evenly stuff all 20 mushrooms with the shrimp mixture.

5) In Instant Pot, evenly coat bottom and up to 1-inch of the side of the pot with oil.
6) Gently put the mushrooms inside the Instant Pot, if needed cook them in two batches.
7) Cover, press the manual button, and adjust cooking time to 2 minutes.
8) Serve and enjoy.

Nutrition information: Calories per serving: 53; Carbohydrates: 1.94g; Protein: 2.85g; Fat: 3.8g; Sugar: 0.86g; Sodium: 224mg; Fiber: 0.4g

23 – Deviled Eggs in Instant Pot

Serves: 5
Cooking Time: 15 minutes
Preparation Time: 15 minutes

Ingredients:
- 5 large eggs
- 1 cup cold water
- Pepper and salt to taste
- ½ teaspoon Sriracha
- 1 teaspoon white vinegar
- 1 teaspoon Dijon mustard
- 1 tablespoon extra-virgin olive oil
- 2 tablespoons full fat mayonnaise
- Spanish Paprika

Instructions:
1) Add water in Instant Pot.
2) Place eggs in steamer basket and put inside Instant Pot.
3) Press manual button, choose low pressure, and adjust cooking time to 12 minutes.
4) Once done cooking, do a quick pressure release.
5) With tongs, transfer eggs into a bowl of cold water.
6) Once eggs are cool enough to handle, peel.

7) Cut eggs in half, lengthwise and remove yolks and place in a medium bowl.

8) In bowl of yolks add Sriracha, white vinegar, mustard, oil, and mayonnaise. Mix well while thoroughly crumbling yolks.

9) Season with pepper and salt to taste.

10) Evenly stuff the egg whites with the yolk mixture.

11) Then sprinkle Spanish Paprika on the tops of the Deviled Eggs.

12) Serve and enjoy.

Nutrition information: Calories per serving: 96; Carbohydrates: 2.14g; Protein: 7.26g; Fat: 6.47g; Sugar: 0.84g; Sodium: 108mg; Fiber: 0.5g

24 – Pan-Fried Portobello Mushrooms Mediterranean Style

Serves: 4
Cooking Time: 6 minutes
Preparation Time: 10 minutes

Ingredients:
- Salt and pepper to taste
- 1 large Portobello Mushroom, sliced into 4 equal slices of at least ½-inch thickness
- ½ teaspoon thyme
- ½ teaspoon basil
- ½ teaspoon tarragon
- ½ teaspoon balsamic vinegar
- 2 tablespoons olive oil

Instructions:
1) In a small bowl, mix well all spices.
2) In Instant Pot, press sauté function and add oil.
3) With pastry brush, brush balsamic vinegar on all sides of the sliced mushroom and season with pepper and salt.
4) In one layer, place mushroom on bottom of pot. If needed, cook in batches.
5) Evenly sprinkle the herb mixture on top of mushrooms.

6) Sauté mushrooms for 3 minutes per side.

Nutrition information: Calories per serving: 70; Carbohydrates: 1.58g; Protein: 1.04g; Fat: 6.94g; Sugar: 0.79g; Sodium: 4 mg; Fiber: 0.7g

25 – Instant Pot Appetizing Meatballs

Serves: 16
Cooking Time: 12 minutes
Preparation Time: 15 minutes

Ingredients:
- 2 tablespoons olive oil
- 2 tablespoons fresh basil, chopped
- ½ cup shredded whole milk mozzarella
- ½ teaspoon garlic powder
- ¼ teaspoon ground black pepper
- ½ teaspoon salt
- ¼ cup almond flour
- 1 egg
- 1-pound ground turkey

Instructions:
1) In a medium bowl, whisk egg.
2) Mix in basil, mozzarella, garlic powder, black pepper, and salt.
3) Add ground turkey ad mix with hands for around 5 minutes, until thoroughly combined.
4) Sprinkle flour and mix once again.
5) Evenly divide mixture into 16 pieces and form into a ball.
6) Press sauté function on Instant Pot.

7) Add oil and in one layer place the meatballs inside the pot. If needed, cook into two batches.
8) Cook the meatballs for 3 minutes per side or until browed all over.

Nutrition information: Calories per serving: 89; Carbohydrates: 0.7g; Protein: 7.39g; Fat: 6.38g; Sugar: 0.19g; Sodium: 118mg; Fiber: 0.3g

Chapter 5 – Instant Pot, Keto Diet Poultry Recipes

26 – Herbed Butter Over Chicken Breast

Serves: 4
Cooking Time: 30 minutes
Preparation Time: 20 minutes

Ingredients:
- ½ teaspoon salt
- 1 teaspoon lemon juice
- 4 tablespoons chopped fresh parsley
- ½ teaspoon garlic powder
- 1 garlic clove
- 1/3-pound butter, at room temperature
- Pepper and salt to taste
- 1-ounce butter
- 4 chicken breast halves
- ½ cup water

Instructions:
1) Make the herbed butter by mixing 1/3-pound butter, garlic clove, garlic powder, lemon juice, and salt in a blender or food processor. Process until smooth and creamy. Mix in chopped fresh parsley and let it sit.

2) Generously season with salt and pepper the chicken.
3) In Instant Pot, press sauté button and heat the 1-ounce butter.
4) Add the seasoned chicken breast and brown each side for 3 minutes. If needed cook in batches.
5) And then return all chicken back to pot.
6) Add water.
7) Cover, press poultry button, and adjust cooking time to 5 minutes.
8) To serve, place chicken breasts on serving plate and evenly slather the herbed butter on top of each breast.

Nutrition information: Calories per serving: 619; Carbohydrates: 0.91g; Protein: 60.47g; Fat: 42.37g; Sugar: 0.11g; Sodium: 682mg; Fiber: 0.2g

27 – Cream Cheese Sauce Over Turkey

Serves: 4
Cooking Time: 50 minutes
Preparation Time: 15 minutes

Ingredients:

- 1 tablespoon Tamari Soy sauce
- 6 ¾ Tablespoons small capers
- Pepper and salt to taste
- 7-ounce cream cheese
- 2 cups sour cream
- 2 tablespoons butter
- 1 1/3-pounds turkey breast
- 1 cup water

Instructions:

1) On Instant Pot, press sauté button.
2) Add a tablespoon of butter and let it melt.
3) Add capers and sauté until crispy, around 8 minutes while constantly stirring them around.
4) Remove and transfer capers to a plate and set aside.
5) Meanwhile season turkey generously with pepper and salt.
6) Add remaining butter to Instant Pot and let it melt.
7) Place turkey in Instant Pot and Brown each side for 3 minutes.

8) After browning turkey breast, add Tamari soy sauce and water.
9) Cover, press poultry button, and adjust cooking time to 20 minutes.
10) Once done cooking, transfer turkey to plate of capers and tent.
11) In same pot, press sauté button and add cream cheese and sour cream.
12) Mix well until thoroughly mixed. Continue cooking until desired consistency is achieved.
13) To serve, pour over turkey meat, slice into ½-inch thick slices, and enjoy.

Nutrition information: Calories per serving: 533; Carbohydrates: 11.23g; Protein: 43.69g; Fat: 35.8g; Sugar: 2.13g; Sodium: 1063mg; Fiber: 0.6g

28 – Chicken Curry Malaysian Style

Serves: 4
Cooking Time: 20 minutes
Preparation Time: 15 minutes

Ingredients:
- Pepper and salt to taste
- 1 tablespoon grated fresh ginger
- 1 red chili pepper, finely chopped
- 1 tablespoon curry paste
- 1 ¾ cups coconut milk
- 3 tablespoons coconut oil
- 1 yellow onion, chopped finely
- 1 red bell pepper
- 1 green bell pepper
- 1-pound chicken thighs, boneless and skinless
- 2 cloves garlic smashed
- 1-inch thumb ginger, sliced into 4 equal pieces
- 1 bay leaf

Instructions:
1) Press sauté button on Instant pot and heat coconut oil.
2) Sauté garlic and ginger until garlic is browned, around 3 minutes.

3) Stir in chopped onions and sauté until soft and translucent, around 5 minutes.
4) Add chili pepper, curry paste, and bay leaf. Sauté for a minute.
5) Stir in chicken, season with pepper and salt generously.
6) Add ½ of the coconut milk.
7) Cover, press poultry button, adjust cooking time to 5 minutes.
8) Do a quick release and stir in bell peppers and remaining coconut milk.
9) Press sauté button and cook for 5 minutes or until coconut milk is heated through.
10) Adjust seasoning to taste with more pepper and salt if needed.
11) Serve and enjoy.

Nutrition information: Calories per serving: 534; Carbohydrates: 9.52g; Protein: 30.96g; Fat: 43.8g; Sugar: 3.03g; Sodium: 192mg; Fiber: 1.9g

29 – Chicken casserole with Olives, Cheese, and Pesto

Serves: 4
Cooking Time: 25 minutes
Preparation Time: 15 minutes

Ingredients:
- 1 tablespoon butter
- Pepper and salt to taste
- 1 garlic clove, chopped finely
- ½-pound feta cheese, diced
- 8 tablespoons pitted olive
- 1 2/3 cups heavy whipping cream
- 3.5-ounce green pesto
- 1.5-pounds chicken breasts

Instructions:
1) Slice chicken breast into 1-inch cubes. Season with pepper and salt.
2) Press sauté button on Instant Pot and heat butter.
3) Add garlic and sauté until browned, around 3 minutes.
4) Add sliced chicken and cook until no longer pink, around 8 minutes.
5) Stir in feta cheese, olives, whipping cream, and green pesto. Stir well.

6) Cover, press poultry setting, and adjust cooking time to 10 minutes.

Nutrition information: Calories per serving: 667; Carbohydrates: 6.11g; Protein: 45.05g; Fat: 51.13g; Sugar: 3.92g; Sodium: 793mg; Fiber: 1g

30 – Chicken Casserole with Tomatoes, Cauliflower, and Pesto

Serves: 6
Cooking Time: 25 minutes
Preparation Time: 15 minutes

Ingredients:
- Pepper and salt to taste
- 3 tablespoons butter
- ½ of a lemon, juiced
- 2 tablespoons green pesto
- 4-ounce cherry tomatoes
- 1 leek, chopped
- 2/3-pounds cauliflower, chopped into bite sized florets
- 1 ¼-cups heavy whipping cream
- 7-ounce shredded cheese
- 2-pounds chicken thighs

Instructions:
1) Press sauté on Instant Pot and heat butter.
2) Add chicken thighs. Eason with pepper and salt.
3) Brown each side for 3 minutes.
4) Add chopped leeks and sauté for a minute.
5) Stir in lemon juice, green pesto, and cherry tomatoes. Cook for a minute.

6) Add cheese, whipping cream, and cauliflower. Mix well.
7) Cover, press poultry button, and adjust cooking time to 15 minutes.

Nutrition information: Calories per serving: 582; Carbohydrates: 9.31g; Protein: 45.75g; Fat: 40g; Sugar: 4.81g; Sodium: 780mg; Fiber: 1.5g

31 – Chicken Stew Belize Style

Serves: 8
Cooking Time: 30 minutes
Preparation Time: 10 minutes

Ingredients:
- 2 cups chicken stock
- 1 tablespoon granulated sugar substitute
- ½ teaspoon ground black pepper
- 1 teaspoon dried oregano
- 1 teaspoon ground cumin
- 3 cloves garlic, sliced
- 1 cup sliced yellow onions
- 3 tablespoons Worcestershire sauce
- 2 tablespoons white vinegar
- 2 tablespoons achiote seasoning
- 1 tablespoon coconut oil
- 4 whole chicken legs, cut into thigh and drumstick pieces

Instructions:
1) Do NOT add salt to this dish.
2) In a large bowl, mix well sweetener, pepper, oregano, cumin, Worcestershire sauce, vinegar, and achiote paste.

3) Add chicken into bowl and rub mix all over chicken. Marinate chicken in the fridge for at least an hour.
4) On Instant Pot, press sauté button. Heat oil.
5) Sauté garlic for a minute. Add onions and continue sautéing for 3 more minutes.
6) Add chicken and cook for 3 minutes per side.
7) Add chicken stock and black pepper.
8) Cover, press manual button, adjust pressure to high, and time for 20 minutes.
9) Do a quick release, serve, and enjoy.

Nutrition information: Calories per serving: 356; Carbohydrates: 12.66g; Protein: 35.8g; Fat: 16.94g; Sugar: 4.68g; Sodium: 581mg; Fiber: 1.2g

32 – Chicken Adobo Filipino Style

Serves: 4
Cooking Time: 25 minutes
Preparation Time: 5 minutes

Ingredients:

- 4-pieces chicken legs, skinless and cut into thigh and drumstick pieces
- ½ cup soy sauce
- 1 tablespoon whole peppercorns
- 4 garlic cloves, smashed and chopped roughly with skin
- 1 medium onion, chopped
- ¼ cup vinegar
- 1 bay leaf
- 1 tablespoon coconut oil

Instructions:

1) Press sauté button on Instant Pot.
2) Add oil and once hot, sauté garlic for 4 minutes or until browned.
3) Add onions and sauté until soft and translucent, around 6 minutes.
4) Add chicken, vinegar, and peppercorn. Bring to a simmer.
5) Turnover chicken and add soy sauce.

6) Cover and press poultry button.
7) Do a quick release.
8) If there is still plenty of liquid in pot, press sauté button and sauté chicken. Turning them over once in a while.
9) Stop sautéing when sauce has thickened.
10) Serve and enjoy.

Nutrition information: Calories per serving: 293; Carbohydrates: 6.98g; Protein: 35.69g; Fat: 13.22g; Sugar: 1.43g; Sodium: 1701mg; Fiber: 1.3g

33 – Lettuce Turkey Wrap

Serves: 4
Cooking Time: 10 minutes
Preparation Time: 10 minutes

Ingredients:
- 12 washed and dried leaves of iceberg or Boston lettuce
- 2 tablespoons honey
- 2 tablespoons lime juice
- 2 tablespoons La Choy Soy Sauce
- ½ cup Peter Pan Crunchy Peanut Butter
- 1 cup water
- 1 cup chopped yellow onion
- 2 cups chopped cooked turkey
- PAM Original No-stick cooking spray

Instructions:
1) Spray Instant Pot with cooking spray and press sauté button.
2) Add yellow onions and sauté for 3 minutes.
3) Stir in chopped turkey and sauté for 3 minutes.
4) Add honey, lime juice, soy sauce, peanut butter, and water. Mix well.
5) Sauté for 3 minutes more and transfer to a plate.

6) To serve, evenly divide turkey mixture into the middle of each lettuce. Roll lettuce and enjoy.

Nutrition information: Calories per serving: 392; Carbohydrates: 20g; Protein: 32g; Fat: 20g; Sugar: 14g; Sodium: 750mg; Fiber: 4g

34 – Keto-Approved Turkey Burger

Serves: 2
Cooking Time: 12 minutes
Preparation Time: 8 minutes

Ingredients:
- ½ teaspoon cumin
- 1 dash pepper
- 1 dash salt
- ¼ teaspoon minced garlic
- ½ teaspoon onion powder
- 4 ½ teaspoons or 1 packet of Dijon mustard
- ½ pound lean ground turkey
- 1 tablespoon olive oil

Instructions:
1) In a bowl, mix all ingredients except for oil. Mix with hands for around 3 minutes.
2) Evenly divide mixture into two and form each into patties.
3) Add oil on Instant Pot and press sauté button.
4) Add turkey patties and cook for 3 minutes per side. If needed, cook patties one at a time.

Nutrition information: Calories per serving: 296; Carbohydrates: 30.28g; Protein: 22.13g; Fat: 9.99g; Sugar: 13.96g; Sodium: 1629mg; Fiber: 1.4g

35 – Chili with Shredded Chicken

Serves: 5
Cooking Time: 25 minutes
Preparation Time: 15 minutes

Ingredients:
- Salt and pepper to taste
- 4 ounces cream cheese, cut into 1-inch cubes
- ½ chopped jalapeno
- ½ tablespoon garlic powder
- 1 tablespoon cumin
- 1 tablespoon chili powder
- ½ can or 3 ounces tomato paste
- 1 (14.5 ounces) can undrained diced tomatoes
- 2 cups chicken broth
- ½ chopped onion
- 1 tablespoon butter
- 2 large shredded chicken breasts

Instructions:
1) On Instant Pot, press sauté button. Add butter and melt.
2) Stir in onions and sauté until soft and translucent, around 5 minutes.
3) Stir in jalapeno, cumin, chili powder, and garlic powder. Sauté for a minute.

4) Stir in tomato paste and dice tomatoes. Mix well.
5) Pour in diced tomatoes and chicken broth. Mix well.
6) Add chicken breasts. Season with pepper and salt.
7) Cover, press poultry button, and adjust cooking time to 10 minutes.
8) Do a quick release.
9) Remove chicken, press sauté button, and stir in cream cheese.
10) While stirring frequently, allow cream cheese to melt.
11) Meanwhile, in a bowl and with forks, shred chicken and then return to pot.
12) Taste and adjust seasoning if needed.
13) When cream cheese is well incorporated, around 10 minutes, serve, and enjoy.

Nutrition information: Calories per serving: 142; Carbohydrates: 10.64g; Protein: 5.03g; Fat: 9.8g; Sugar: 6.24g; Sodium: 641mg; Fiber: 2.6g

Chapter 6 – Instant Pot, Keto Diet Meat Recipes

36 – Mushroom Bacon Cheeseburger Lettuce Wraps

Serves: 4
Cooking Time: 30 minutes
Preparation Time: 15 minutes

Ingredients:
- 1 iceberg lettuce, washed and separated leaves
- 1 cup shredded cheddar cheese
- ¼ teaspoon pepper
- ½ teaspoon salt
- 1 ½-pounds ground beef
- 3 ½-ounces sliced mushroom
- 12 slices of bacon
- Salt and pepper to taste

Instructions:
1) On Instant Pot, press sauté button and cook bacon until crisped, around 4 minutes per side. If needed, cook in batches.
2) Place crisped bacon on a plate, crumble or chop into 1-inch, and set aside.

3) In pot with bacon grease, add mushrooms and sauté until soft, around 7 minutes.
4) Transfer mushrooms to a plate or bowl.
5) Add ground beef, season with pepper and salt, and cook until no longer pink, around 10 minutes.
6) Transfer cooked ground beef to a plate or bowl.
7) To serve, in one lettuce leaf add in the middle ground beef, sprinkle cheese, followed by mushrooms, and lastly the crumbled bacon.
8) Roll leaf and enjoy wrap.

Nutrition information: Calories per serving: 924; Carbohydrates: 14.68g; Protein: 66.13g; Fat: 65.97g; Sugar: 9.8g; Sodium: 1723mg; Fiber: 1.9g

37 – Red Pesto Chops

Serves: 4
Cooking Time: 10 minutes
Preparation Time: 10 minutes

Ingredients:

- ⅓-pound mayonnaise
- 2 to 4 tablespoons red pesto, for dip
- 4 tablespoons red pesto for marinating
- 2 tablespoons butter or olive oil
- 4 pork chops
- ½ cup water

Instructions:

1) Rub 1 tablespoon red pesto per chop. Let it sit for at least 10 minutes.
2) Meanwhile, make the dip by mixing mayonnaise and 2 tablespoons red pesto. Mix well and adjust red pesto to taste by adding more if desired.
3) On Instant Pot, press sauté button and heat oil.
4) Once oil is hot, around 4 minutes, add pork chops and brown for 2 minutes per side.
5) Add ½ cup water, cover, press manual button, choose high pressure, and time for 3 minutes.
6) Serve and enjoy with the dipping sauce.

Nutrition information: Calories per serving: 577; Carbohydrates: 0.64g; Protein: 41.94g; Fat: 44.26g; Sugar: 0.13g; Sodium: 593mg; Fiber: 0.2g

38 – Herbed and Buttered Lamb Chops

Serves: 4
Cooking Time: 10 minutes
Preparation Time: 20 minutes

Ingredients:
- Herbed Butter
- Salt
- Pepper
- 1 lemon, sliced into wedges
- 1 tablespoon olive oil
- 1 tablespoon butter
- 8 lamb chops

Herbed Butter Ingredients:
- 1 stick butter (8 tablespoons)
- 1 medium garlic clove, peeled and smashed
- 1 teaspoon garlic powder
- 2 tablespoons fresh parsley
- ¼ teaspoon lemon juice
- A dash of salt

Instructions:
1) Season lamb chops with pepper and salt generously. Set aside to marinate for a bit.

2) In a microwave safe bowl, melt butter in 30-second bursts. Be careful as melting butter in microwave too long will cause splattering.

3) Once butter is melted, pour into food processor and add garlic clove. Process until garlic is fine and pureed.

4) Mix in garlic powder, lemon juice, and salt. Process for 30 seconds or until thoroughly mixed.

5) Add fresh parsley and pulse 2 to 3 times.

6) Pour herbed butter into a mold or bowl and stash in the fridge until ready to use.

7) On Instant Pot, press sauté button and heat olive oil and 1 tablespoon butter.

8) Fry the lamb chops for 3 to 5 minutes per side, depending on how you want it.

9) Serve with the herbed butter and enjoy.

Nutrition information: Calories per serving: 385; Carbohydrates: 1.96g; Protein: 17.26g; Fat: 35.01g; Sugar: 1.12g; Sodium: 313mg; Fiber: 0.3g

39 – Keto Approved Beef Stroganoff

Serves: 4
Cooking Time: 20 minutes
Preparation Time: 10 minutes

Ingredients:
- 1 ½ cups sour cream
- ½ pound blue cheese
- 1 pinch ground black pepper
- ½ teaspoon salt
- 1 tablespoon dried thyme
- ½ pound mushrooms
- 1 yellow onion, chopped
- 3 tablespoons butter
- 1 pound ground beef
- 2 zucchinis, peeled and spiralized

Instructions:
1) On Instant Pot, press sauté button and heat butter.
2) Once butter is melted, stir in onions and sauté until soft and translucent, around 5 minutes.
3) Add beef and sauté for 8 minutes. Season with salt and pepper.
4) Stir in sour cream blue cheese, and thyme.
5) Cover, press manual button, choose low pressure, and cook for 5 minutes.

6) To serve, evenly divide spiralized zucchini on to 4 plates, and top with ¼ of the stroganoff mixture.

Nutrition information: Calories per serving: 726; Carbohydrates: 11.81g; Protein: 45.96g; Fat: 55.02g; Sugar: 2.57g; Sodium: 11.62mg; Fiber: 1.3g

40 – Blue Cheese Sauce Pork Chops

Serves: 4
Cooking Time: 30 minutes
Preparation Time: 10 minutes

Ingredients:
- 3 tablespoons butter, divided
- 7-ounce green beans
- 1 ¼ cups sour cream
- 7-ounce blue cheese
- Pepper and salt to taste
- 4 pork chops

Instructions:
1) Season pork chops with pepper and salt. Set aside.
2) Press sauté function on Instant Pot and heat 1 tablespoon butter.
3) Sauté green beans until soft, around 7 to 10 minutes. Season with pepper and salt. Once done, transfer to a plate and keep warm.
4) Add a tablespoon of butter and once melted, pan fry pork chops for 4 minutes per side. Transfer to plates, tent, and keep warm.
5) Add remaining butter in Instant Pot, and add cheese. Crumble as you melt it. Once melted, stir in sour

cream. Continue cooking until mixture is heated through. Transfer to a gravy boat and serve as a dip.

Nutrition information: Calories per serving: 721; Carbohydrates: 8.36g; Protein: 56.51g; Fat: 50.63g; Sugar: 0.86g; Sodium: 814mg; Fiber: 0.9g

41 – Béarnaise Sauce over Steak

Serves: 4
Cooking Time: 15 minutes
Preparation Time: 15 minutes

Ingredients:
- Salt
- Pepper
- 2/3-pound butter
- 2 tablespoons finely chopped fresh tarragon
- 2 pinches onion powder
- 2 teaspoons white wine vinegar
- 4 egg yolks
- 2 tablespoons butter
- 4 ribeye steaks

Instructions:
1) To make the sauce, separate yolk from whites and discard whites.
2) In a heat resistant bowl, place yolks.
3) In another bowl mix tarragon, onion powder, and vinegar.
4) In a microwave safe bowl, place 2/3-pound butter. Slice butter into ¼-inch thick slices and spread. Microwave for 30-seconds, mix, microwave for

another 30 seconds more. Mix well. And if needed, microwave in bursts of 10-seconds each time.

5) Pour melted butter into egg yolk as you whisk the eggs vigorously while slowly pouring in melted butter.

6) Then, whisk in the bowl of vinegar mixture into bowl of eggs, while whisking constantly. Keep Béarnaise sauce warm.

7) Season steaks generously with pepper and salt.

8) On Instant Pot, press sauté function and add 2 tablespoons butter and let it melt.

9) Add ribeye steaks and cook for 3 minutes per side for medium.

10) Serve with warm Béarnaise sauce on the side.

Nutrition information: Calories per serving: 721; Carbohydrates: 8.36g; Protein: 56.51g; Fat: 50.63g; Sugar: 0.86g; Sodium: 814mg; Fiber: 0.9g

42 – Patties with Tomato Sauce and Fried Cabbage

Serves: 4
Cooking Time: 15 minutes
Preparation Time: 10 minutes

Ingredients:
- 1 ounce butter
- 1 tablespoon olive oil
- 1 ¾ ounce finely chopped fresh parsley
- ¼ teaspoon ground black pepper
- 1 teaspoon salt
- 3 ¼ ounce feta cheese
- 1 egg
- 1 ½ pounds ground beef
- 4 ¼ ounce butter
- 1 ½ pounds shredded green cabbage

Instructions:
1) In a large bowl, mix parsley, ¼ teaspoon pepper, 1 teaspoon salt, cheese, egg, and ground beef. Mix well with hands.
2) On Instant Pot, press sauté button and heat 4 ¼-ounce butter. Once melted stir in green cabbage and season with pepper and salt.

3) Sauté for 5 minutes or until desired wilting of cabbage is achieved. Transfer to a bowl and keep warm.
4) While veggie is cooking, divide ground beef into 4 equal portions and make a pattie out of each.
5) In same pot, add an ounce of butter and 1 tablespoon olive oil.
6) Once hot, pan fry patties for 4 minutes per side.
7) Serve with a side of buttered cabbage and enjoy.

Nutrition information: Calories per serving: 1017; Carbohydrates: 14.35g; Protein: 51.88g; Fat: 84.37g; Sugar: 7.81g; Sodium: 1664mg; Fiber: 4.3g

43 – Cabbage Stir-Fry Indian Style

Serves: 4
Cooking Time: 25 minutes
Preparation Time: 10 minutes

Ingredients:
- 1 cup mayonnaise
- 8 tablespoons fresh cilantro
- ½ finely chopped yellow onion
- 1 tablespoon red curry paste
- 1 tablespoon white wine vinegar
- 1 teaspoon onion powder
- ¼ teaspoon ground black pepper
- 1 teaspoon salt
- 1 1/3 pounds ground pork/lamb
- 1/3-pound butter
- 1 2/3 pounds green cabbage

Instructions:
1) Add cabbage in food processor and shred as finely as you can.
2) In Instant Pot, press sauté button and melt half of the butter.
3) Add shredded cabbage and fry for 6 minutes or until soft.

4) Stir in vinegar and onion powder. Mix well. Then transfer cabbage to a plate and set aside.
5) In same pot, melt remaining butter and sauté garlic for a minute.
6) Stir in onion and sauté for 3 minutes.
7) Add curry paste and sauté for a minute.
8) Stir in meat and cook for 10 minutes.
9) Add back cabbage in to pot, mix well, season with pepper and salt.
10) Cook for another minute, serve and enjoy.

Nutrition information: Calories per serving: 976; Carbohydrates: 14.81g; Protein: 41.35g; Fat: 84.11g; Sugar: 7.31g; Sodium: 1902mg; Fiber: 4.8g

44 – Moroccan Beef Slow Cooked

Serves: 8
Cooking Time: 8 hours
Preparation Time: 5 minutes

Ingredients:
- 1 teaspoon sea salt
- 4 tablespoons garam masala seasoning
- 2 pounds beef roast
- ½ cup sliced yellow onions
- 2 cups water
- ½ cup apricots

Instructions:
1) Rub salt and garam masala all over roast beef.
2) Place onions and apricots on bottom of Instant Pot.
3) Place roast beef on top of onions and apricots.
4) Pour water.
5) Cover, press slow cook button, adjust cooking time to 6 hours.
6) Once done cooking, remove roast beef and shred with 2 forks.
7) Return to pot, cover, press slow cook and adjust time to 2 hours.
8) Serve and enjoy.

Nutrition information: Calories per serving: 275; Carbohydrates: 3.04g; Protein: 31.89g; Fat: 14.72g; Sugar: 0.75g; Sodium: 997mg; Fiber: 0.7g

45 – Tex-Mex Casserole Keto Style

Serves: 4
Cooking Time: 15 minutes
Preparation Time: 10 minutes

Ingredients:
- 2 ounces butter
- 1 finely chopped scallion, finely chopped
- 1 cup sour cream
- 7 ounces shredded cheese
- 2 ounces pickled jalapenos
- 7 ounces crushed tomatoes
- 1 ½ pounds ground beef
- A pinch of cayenne
- 2 teaspoons onion powder
- 1 teaspoon ground cumin
- 2 teaspoons paprika
- 2 teaspoons chili powder

Instructions:
1) Press sauté button on Instant Pot and heat butter.
2) Add ground beef and sauté for 8 minutes or until no longer pink.
3) Add tomatoes, cayenne, onion powder, cumin, paprika, and chili powder. Sauté for another minute.
4) Press warm button.

5) Evenly spread ground beef on bottom of pot, add shredded cheese evenly on top of beef.
6) Then evenly top with jalapenos.
7) Cover, press manual button, low pressure, and cooking time for 2 minutes.
8) Meanwhile, mix sour cream and scallion in a bowl. Mix well.
9) Serve sour cream mixture on the side.

Nutrition information: Calories per serving: 861; Carbohydrates: 6.94g; Protein: 69.83g; Fat: 60.3g; Sugar: 1g; Sodium: 683mg; Fiber: 0.8g

46 – Pressure cooked lamb shanks

Serves: 4
Cooking Time: 1 hour 10 minutes
Preparation Time: 25 minutes

Ingredients:
- ¼ cup minced Italian parsley
- 1 tablespoon aged balsamic vinegar
- 1 teaspoon red boat fish sauce
- 1 cup bone broth
- 1 pound ripe roma tomatoes or 1 (14ounce) can drained diced tomatoes
- 3 cloves smashed and peeled garlic
- 1 tablespoon tomato paste
- 1 large onion roughly chopped
- 2 celery stalks, roughly chopped
- 2 medium carrots, roughly chopped
- 2 tablespoon divided ghee
- Freshly ground black pepper
- Kosher salt
- 3 pounds lamb shank

Instructions:
1) Season lamb with pepper and salt.
2) On Instant Pot, heat 1 tablespoon ghee and once hot, add lamb and brown sides for 5 minutes per side.

3) Transfer lamb to a plate.
4) Add remaining ghee.
5) Once ghee is hot, stir in onion, celery, and carrots. Season with pepper and salt. Sauté for 8 minutes or until translucent.
6) Stir in garlic cloves and tomato paste. Mix well and sauté for a minute.
7) Return shanks to pot.
8) Add tomatoes, fish sauce, bone broth, more pepper, and balsamic vinegar.
9) Cover, press cancel button, press manual button, choose high pressure, and time for 50 minutes.
10) To serve, sprinkle Italian parsley.

Nutrition information: Calories per serving: 474; Carbohydrates: 13.1g; Protein: 77.19g; Fat: 13.29g; Sugar: 7.24g; Sodium: 601mg; Fiber: 4.1g

47 – Goat Curry

Serves: 4
Cooking Time: hours minutes
Preparation Time: minutes

Ingredients:
- ½ pound potatoes
- ½ cup water
- 1 teaspoon garam masala
- 2 (14 ounce) cans organic diced tomatoes
- 1 teaspoon paprika
- 1 teaspoon Kashmiri chili powder
- 1 teaspoon turmeric powder
- 2 teaspoons salt
- 1 teaspoon cumin powder
- 1 tablespoon coriander powder
- 4 cardamom pods
- 4 cloves
- 1 bay leaf
- 3 cloves garlic, peeled, smashed, and chopped
- 1 ½ inch knob fresh ginger
- 2 onions, chopped
- 2 pounds goat meat
- 2 tablespoons avocado oil

Instructions:

1) Press sauté button on Instant Pot, and heat oil.
2) Once oil is hot, brown goat meat for 10 minutes.
3) Add garlic, ginger, and onions. Sauté for 5 minutes.
4) Stir in paprika, Kashmiri, turmeric, salt, cumin, coriander, cardamom pods, cloves, garam masala, and bay leaf. Sauté for 2 minutes.
5) Add potatoes, water, and diced tomatoes. Mix well.
6) Cover, press cancel button, press meat/stew button, and increase time to 45 minutes.
7) Do a natural release method, then serve and enjoy.

Nutrition information: Calories per serving: 477; Carbohydrates: 19.94g; Protein: 64.6g; Fat: 14.49g; Sugar: 3.12g; Sodium: 1415mg; Fiber: 3.6g

48 – Slow Cooked Lamb the Keto Way

Serves: 4
Cooking Time: 8 hours
Preparation Time: 20 minutes

Ingredients:
- Salt
- Pepper
- ¾ teaspoon garlic
- ¾ teaspoon dried rosemary
- 6-7 mint leaves
- 4 sprigs thyme
- 1 tablespoon maple syrup
- 2 tablespoons whole grain mustard
- ¼ cup olive oil
- 2 pounds lamb leg

Instructions:
1) Make a total of 3 slits of 1 ½-inch deep on the lamb.
2) Rub the following seasoning all over the lamb: pepper and salt to taste, maple syrup, and whole grain mustard.
3) Then insert rosemary and garlic into each slit.
4) Place lamb in Instant pot.
5) Add olive oil.

6) Cover, press slow cook button, choose low pressure, and time for 7 hours.
7) Do a quick release.
8) Add mint, thyme, cover, press slow cook button, choose low pressure, and time for an hour.
9) Then serve and enjoy.

Nutrition information: Calories per serving: 495; Carbohydrates: 16.92g; Protein: 48.98g; Fat: 26.29g; Sugar: 3.62g; Sodium: 153mg; Fiber: 6g

49 – Mutton Curry Keto

Serves: 2
Cooking Time: hours minutes
Preparation Time: minutes

Ingredients:
- 2 bay leaves
- 1 black cardamom
- 1 pinch of asafetida, optional
- 4 cloves of garlic
- 10 green cardamoms
- 1 stick of cinnamon
- 1 ½ teaspoons cumin seeds
- ½ teaspoon of cumin powder
- ½ teaspoon of garam masala
- 1/3 teaspoon turmeric powder
- 2 teaspoons of coriander powder
- 1/3 teaspoon cayenne pepper powder
- 1/3 teaspoon black pepper powder
- Salt
- 100 ml ghee
- Handful of freshly chopped coriander
- 1 tablespoon of freshly garlic paste
- 1 tablespoon of fresh ginger paste
- 1 chopped large red tomato
- 2-3 chopped Asian green chilies

- 1 finely chopped medium onion
- 600 grams goat meat on bones

Instructions:
1) Press sauté button on Instant Pot and heat ghee.
2) Sauté cumin seeds, cloves, cardamoms, cinnamon, cumin seeds, bay leaves, and asafetida if using. Sauté for 3 minutes.
3) Add green chillies and chopped onions. Sauté for 5 minutes.
4) Add garlic paste and ginger. Sauté for 2 minutes.
5) Add tomatoes and cook for 5 minutes or until mushy.
6) Add cayenne, cumin powder, coriander powder, black pepper powder, salt, and turmeric powder. Sauté for a minute.
7) Add meat and cook for 6 minutes. If there is too much browning, you can add ½ cup of water.
8) Add 1 ½ cups of water, cover, press cancel button, press meat/stew button, and adjust time to 20 minutes.
9) Do a quick release. Stir in garam masala and mix well.
10) To serve, garnish with freshly chopped coriander.

Nutrition information: Calories per serving: 752; Carbohydrates: 48.24g; Protein: 95.91g; Fat: 21.12g; Sugar: 5.94g; Sodium: 1639mg; Fiber: 11.8g

50 – Protein Noodle Lasagna

Serves: 12
Cooking Time: 4 hours 15 minutes
Preparation Time: 30 minutes

Ingredients:
- ½ pound sliced deli chicken breast
- ¾ cup parmesan cheese
- ¾ sliced mozzarella cheese
- ½ teaspoon sea salt
- 1 egg
- 1 pound ricotta cheese
- 1 ½ pounds unsweetened marinara sauce
- ½ yellow onion, chopped
- 1 clove garlic, peeled, smashed, and chopped
- ¾ pound ground beef
- 1 pound Italian sausages, sliced into ½-inch thick slices

Instructions:
1) On Instant Pot, spray sides and bottom generously with cooking spray and press sauté function.
2) Sauté garlic for a minute. Add chopped onion and sauté for 2 minutes.

3) Stir in ground beef and cook for 5 minutes or until no longer pink.
4) Add Italian sausages and cook for another 5 minutes.
5) Stir in Marinara sauce, mix well, and cook for 3 minutes or until heated through.
6) Transfer sauce to a large bowl.
7) Wipe inner pot clean and generously spray with cooking spray the sides and bottom of pot. Press warm button.
8) Meanwhile, in a bowl mix well salt, egg, and ricotta cheese.
9) To assemble, in bottom of pot evenly spread 1 cup of marinara sauce, top with 1 layer of sliced deli chicken, top with half of the ricotta cheese mixture, top with 1/3 of the mozzarella cheese slices. Then repeat the layering process one more time.
10) Cover, press slow cooker function, and this will take 4 hours of cooking.
11) Serve and enjoy. If you want browned tops, you can torch the top.

Nutrition information: Calories per serving: 356; Carbohydrates: 7.45g; Protein: 23.64g; Fat: 25.3g; Sugar: 3.56g; Sodium: 975mg; Fiber: 1.1g

Chapter 7 – Instant Pot, Keto Diet Soup Recipes

51 – Easy Lobster Bisque in Instant Pot

Serves: 4
Cooking Time: 7 hours and 45 minutes
Preparation Time: 45 minutes

Ingredients:
- 2 cups heavy whipping cream
- 4 whole lobster tails
- ½ teaspoon paprika
- 1 teaspoon ground black pepper
- ¼ cup fresh parsley chopped
- 1 teaspoon dried dill
- 1 tablespoon old bay seasoning
- 32-ounces low sodium chicken broth
- 29-ounces canned petite diced tomatoes with juice
- 1 clove garlic, minced finely
- 2 whole shallots, minced finely
- I teaspoon oil

Instructions:
1) Press sauté button in Instant Pot.
2) Add oil.

116

3) Sauté garlic and shallots. Cook until shallots are starting to look translucent and wilted, around 2 to 3 minutes.
4) Press slow cook button and set pressure of Instant Pot to low.
5) Add paprika, pepper, parsley, dill, old bay seasoning, chicken broth, and tomatoes into Instant Pot.
6) Mix well. Cover and cook for 6 hours.
7) And then with an immersion blender, puree the mixture inside the Instant Pot to desired creaminess.
8) Add lobster tails, cover and cook for an hour or until shells turn red.
9) Remove lobster tails from pot and place on a plate to cool.
10) Meanwhile, stir in whipping cream into Instant Pot and mix well.
11) Cover Instant Pot and continue to cook for 30 minutes.
12) Then, remove as much as you can the lobster tail flesh from its shell. Chop the flesh to desired chunks.
13) Add chopped lobster flesh back into Instant Pot, mix well, and serve.

Nutrition information: Calories per serving: 405; Carbohydrates: 7.75g; Protein: 42.86g; Fat: 21.72g; Sugar: 4.26g; Sodium: 1045mg; Fiber: 1.4g

52 – Coconut-Mussels Thai Style

Serves: 4
Cooking Time: 20 minutes
Preparation Time: 15 minutes

Ingredients:
- 1 tablespoon lime juice
- Zest of 1 lime
- ½ cup fresh cilantro leaves
- 1 ½ cups unsweetened coconut milk
- 2-pounds fresh mussels, cleaned, scrubbed, and debearded
- 1 shallot, minced
- 1 stalk lemongrass, smashed with knife
- 1 small Thai bird Chile, chopped
- 2 cloves garlic, grated with a rasp grater
- 1 tablespoon fish sauce, plus more if needed
- 1 cup chicken broth
- 1 teaspoon oil

Instructions:
1) Set Instant Pot to sauté.
2) Add oil and once hot, add in shallot, lemongrass, Chile, and garlic. Sauté for at least 5 minutes or until shallots are translucent.

3) Stir in fish sauce and chicken stock. Bring to a simmer.
4) Stir in coconut milk.
5) Add the mussels.
6) Cover and press steam function.
7) Steam cook for 10 minutes or until they open.
8) Discard unopened mussels.
9) Mix well and adjust seasoning to taste.
10) Serve and enjoy.

Nutrition information: Calories per serving: 384; Carbohydrates: 15g; Protein: 30.45g; Fat: 23.43g; Sugar: 0.96g; Sodium: 1253mg; Fiber: 0.3g

53 – Leek and Broccoli Creamy Soup

Serves: 4
Cooking Time: 30 minutes
Preparation Time: 10 minutes

Ingredients:
- Salt
- Pepper
- ½ clove of garlic
- 8 tablespoons fresh basil
- 3-ounces butter or olive oil
- 3 ½ cups water
- ½-pound cream cheese
- 2/3-pound broccoli
- 1 leek

Instructions:
1) Cut core of broccoli and slice thinly. Then cut into small florets.
2) Chop leeks finely.
3) On Instant Pot, add broccoli and leeks.
4) Add remaining ingredients except for cream cheese.
5) Cover and press soup button.
6) Do a quick release, stir in cream cheese.
7) With an immersion blender, puree soup until smooth and creamy.

8) If too thick, add more water to desired thickness.

Nutrition information: Calories per serving: 276; Carbohydrates: 7.58g; Protein: 7.04g; Fat: 25.2g; Sugar: 3.16g; Sodium: 490mg; Fiber: 2.6g

54 – Turkey Asian Soup with Cilantro Butter

Serves: 4
Cooking Time: 50 minutes
Preparation Time: 10 minutes

Ingredients:
- 1 tablespoon lime juice
- ½ teaspoon crushed coriander seeds
- 4 ounces butter
- 1/3 cup chopped fresh cilantro
- 2 tablespoons olive oil
- 4-ounces fresh green beans
- ½ teaspoon pepper
- 2 teaspoons salt
- 2 cups water
- 27-ounces coconut milk
- 1 green/yellow bell pepper
- 1 tablespoon green curry paste
- 1-pound ground turkey or chicken
- 1-ounce grated fresh ginger, grate
- 1 yellow onion, chop
- 3 tablespoons coconut oil

Instructions:
1) On Instant Pot, press sauté button and heat oil.

2) Once oil is hot, sauté grated ginger for a minute then add onions and continue sautéing for another 5 minutes.
3) Add bell peppers and curry paste, cook for 3 minutes.
4) Add pepper, coriander seeds, salt, butter, turkey, and coconut milk.
5) Cover, press soup button.
6) Do a quick release.
7) Stir in lime juice, cilantro, and green beans. Mix well and wait for 5 minutes before serving.

Nutrition information: Calories per serving: 1008; Carbohydrates: 16.46g; Protein: 27.91g; Fat: 97.07g; Sugar: 7.83g; Sodium: 2029mg; Fiber: 6.4g

55 – Mushroom Cream Soup

Serves: 5
Cooking Time: 30 minutes
Preparation Time: 5 minutes

Ingredients:
- ¼ teaspoon black pepper
- ¾ sea salt
- 1 cup unsweetened almond milk or coconut milk
- 1 cup heavy cream
- 2 cups chicken broth
- 6 cloves of garlic
- 20-ounces mushroom
- ½ large onion
- 1 tablespoon olive oil

Instructions:
1) On Instant Pot, add all ingredients except for heavy cream.
2) Cover and press soup button.
3) Do a quick release.
4) With an immersion blender, puree soup.
5) Stir in heavy cream.
6) Serve and enjoy.

Nutrition information: Calories per serving: 484; Carbohydrates: 93.76g; Protein: 12.7g; Fat: 13.55g; Sugar: g; Sodium: 452mg; Fiber: 13.6g

56 – Low Carb Cabbage Roll Soup

Serves: 9
Cooking Time: 35 minutes
Preparation Time: 10 minutes

Ingredients:
- 1 large cabbage, cut into quarter
- 5 cups beef broth
- ½ head cauliflower chopped finely or 2 cups riced cauliflower
- 16 ounces marinara sauce
- 1 teaspoon pepper
- 1 teaspoon salt
- ½ teaspoon dried oregano
- 1 teaspoon dried parsley
- 2 pounds ground beef
- ½ cup chopped shallots
- ½ cup chopped onion
- 2 garlic cloves
- 2 tablespoons extra virgin olive oil

Instructions:
1) On Instant Pot, press sauté button and heat oil.
2) Sauté garlic for a minute. Add shallots and onions and sauté for 3 minutes.

3) Add ground beef, sauté until browned, around 8 minutes.
4) Pour in broth, marinara sauce, pepper, salt, oregano, and parsley. Mix well.
5) Add cabbage and cauliflower, mix well.
6) Cover, press cancel button, press soup button, and adjust cooking time to 20 minutes.
7) Do a quick release, then serve and enjoy.

Nutrition information: Calories per serving: 429; Carbohydrates: 18.11g; Protein: 30.63g; Fat: 20.27g; Sugar: 8.25g; Sodium: 1095mg; Fiber: 5.3g

57 – Ground beef and peppers in Goulash Soup

Serves: 7
Cooking Time: 25 minutes
Preparation Time: 20 minutes

Ingredients:
- 2 cans (14.5-ounces) petite diced tomatoes
- 4 cups homemade beef stock
- ½ teaspoon hot paprika
- 2 tablespoon sweet paprika
- 1 tablespoon minced garlic
- 1 large onion, julienned
- 1 large red bell pepper, julienned
- 3 teaspoon olive oil
- 1 1/2-pounds extra lean ground beef

Instructions:
1) Press sauté button on Instant Pot and heat 2 teaspoon oil.
2) Add ground beef and sauté for 8 minutes or until browned. Transfer to a bowl.
3) Add remaining oil into pot and stir fry onions and bell pepper, for 2 minutes.
4) Add hot paprika, sweet paprika, and garlic. Cook for 3 minutes more.

5) Add back beef. Add tomatoes and broth. Mix well.
6) Cover, press cancel button, press manual button, choose low pressure, and time for 15 minutes.
7) Do a quick release, then serve and enjoy.

Nutrition information: Calories per serving: 322; Carbohydrates: 12.07g; Protein: 26.97g; Fat: 18.27g; Sugar: 2.12g; Sodium: 961mg; Fiber: 2.5g

58 – Chicken Green Chili

Serves: 5
Cooking Time: 35 minutes
Preparation Time: 10 minutes

Ingredients:
- 1 tablespoon Asian fish sauce
- ½ cup loosely packed fresh cilantro
- Kosher Salt
- 1 tablespoon whole cumin seed
- 6 medium cloves of garlic
- 10-ounces white onion
- 2 serrano or jalapeno chilies
- 6-ounces Anaheim or Cubanelle peppers
- 1-pound poblano peppers
- ¾-pound tomatillos
- 3-pounds chicken thighs and drumsticks

Instructions:
1) On Instant Pot, add a big pinch of salt, cumin, garlic, onion, serrano peppers, Anaheim peppers, poblano peppers, tomatillos, and chicken.
2) Cover and press soup button.
3) Do a quick release.
4) Remove chicken from pot and shred with 2 forks.

5) Add fish sauce and cilantro into Instant Pot and puree with an immersion blender.
6) Taste and adjust seasoning if needed.
7) Return chicken to pot, mix well, serve and enjoy.

Nutrition information: Calories per serving: 1080; Carbohydrates: 64.49g; Protein: 55.84g; Fat: 64.94g; Sugar: 10.42g; Sodium: 2411mg; Fiber: 4.9g

59 – Keto Style Zuppa Toscana

Serves: 6
Cooking Time: 25 minutes
Preparation Time: 15 minutes

Ingredients:

- Salt
- Pepper
- ½ cup full-fat coconut milk or heavy cream
- 2 cups chopped fresh kale
- 1 teaspoon dried fennel
- 2 teaspoons dried basil
- 5 cups chicken broth
- 3 large russet potatoes
- 1-pound Italian sausage
- 3 cloves garlic
- 1 medium yellow onion
- 2 tablespoons olive/avocado oil

Instructions:

1) Press sauté button and add oil.
2) Sauté garlic for a minute.
3) Add sausages and sauté for 5 minutes.
4) Press cancel button.
5) Add potatoes, herbs, and chicken broth.

6) Cover, press soup button, and adjust cooking time to 15 minutes.
7) Do a quick release.
8) Stir in kale, heavy cream, and mix well.
9) Season with pepper and salt to taste.
10) Add crushed red pepper, mix well, serve, and enjoy.

Nutrition information: Calories per serving: 532; Carbohydrates: 38.25g; Protein: 17.08g; Fat: 32.25g; Sugar: 3.48g; Sodium: 1365mg; Fiber: 3.5g

60 – Instant Pot Seafood Medley Stew

Serves: 6
Cooking Time: 25 minutes
Preparation Time: 5 minutes

Ingredients:
- 2-pounds seafood medley (crab legs, shrimps, scallops, mussels, squid, fish)
- A pinch of cayenne, optional
- ¼ teaspoon red pepper flakes
- ½ teaspoon pepper
- ½ teaspoon salt
- ½ teaspoon celery salt
- 1 teaspoon dried cilantro
- 1 teaspoon dried basil
- 1 teaspoon dried thyme
- ½ medium onion, diced
- 3 cloves minced garlic
- 4 cups vegetable broth
- 1 can crushed tomatoes

Instructions:
1) Press sauté.
2) Heat oil and once hot sauté garlic for a minute or until lightly browned.
3) Stir in onion and sauté until soft, around 5 minutes.

4) Stir in cayenne (if using), red pepper flakes, pepper, salt, celery salt, cilantro, basil, and thyme. Sauté for a minute.
5) Pour in crushed tomatoes and cook until heated through, around 5 minutes.
6) Add vegetable broth and seafood medley.
7) Cover, press steam button and cook for 10 minutes.

Nutrition information: Calories per serving: 357; Carbohydrates: 5.1g; Protein: 28.54g; Fat: 14.44g; Sugar: 2.84g; Sodium: 890mg; Fiber: 0.9g

Chapter 8 – Instant Pot, Keto Diet Seafood Recipes

61 – Poached and Herbed Salmon

Serves: 4
Cooking Time: 3 minutes
Preparation Time: 15 minutes

Ingredients:
- 1 tablespoon olive oil
- ½ lemon, sliced into wedges
- Salt and pepper to taste
- 2-pounds skin on salmon fillet
- 1 teaspoon salt
- 1 teaspoon peppercorns
- 6 sprigs fresh herbs like Italian parsley, dill or tarragon
- 1 bay leaf
- 1 shallot, sliced thinly
- 1 lemon, sliced thinly
- 2 cups water

Instructions:
1) Pour water into inner pot of Instant Pot.

2) Stir in salt, peppercorns, herbs, bay leaf, and shallots.
3) Evenly spread the thinly sliced lemon on bottom of pot.
4) Season salmon with pepper and salt.
5) Then place on top of lemons with skin side down.
6) Cover, press steam function, adjust time to 3 minutes and cook.
7) To serve, drizzle with oil and place lemon wedges on the side.

Nutrition information: Calories per serving: 504; Carbohydrates: 1.5g; Protein: 46.5g; Fat: 30.5g; Sugar: 0.4g; Sodium: 723.4mg; Fiber: 0.2g

62 – Slow-Cooked Garlic-Herbed Mussels

Serves: 5
Cooking Time: 10 minutes
Preparation Time: 20 minutes

Ingredients:
- ¾ cup water
- A dash of red pepper flakes
- 1 teaspoon paprika
- ½ teaspoon black pepper
- ½ tablespoon basil
- 2 tablespoons oregano
- 1 14.5-ounce cans of diced tomatoes
- 8-ounce mushrooms, diced
- 4 cloves garlic, minced
- 3 tablespoons olive oil
- 2.5-pounds mussels

Instructions:
1) Clean mussels by scrubbing and debearding.
2) Press sauté function on In Instant Pot.
3) Heat olive oil and sauté garlic until pungent and lightly browned, around 2 minutes.
4) Add mushrooms and cook for two minutes.
5) Except for the mussels, add the rest of the ingredients into pot and sauté for a minute more.

6) Add cleaned mussels into Instant Pot. Mix well.
7) Cover, press the steam button and adjust time to 4 minutes.
8) Once done cooking, do a quick release, and discard unopened mussels.
9) Serve and enjoy.

Nutrition information: Calories per serving: 497; Carbohydrates: 24.08g; Protein: 56g; Fat: 18.82g; Sugar: 3.55g; Sodium: 947.2mg; Fiber: 3.36g

63 – Instant Pot Poached Lemon & Herb Cod

Serves: 4
Cooking Time: 2 minutes
Preparation Time: 5 minutes

Ingredients:
- Fresh lemons for garnish
- ¼ cup water
- ½ lemon, juiced
- 2 tablespoons Herbs de Provence
- 4 cod fillets, frozen

Instructions:
1) Place cod fillets in Instant Pot, preferably in a single layer.
2) Season cod with Herbs de Provence. If preferred, you can also season with pepper and salt.
3) Squirt lemon juice on fish.
4) Cover, press steam function, adjust cooking time to 2 minutes.
5) To serve, garnish tops of cod with lemon slices.

Nutrition information: Calories per serving: 81; Carbohydrates: 1.26g; Protein: 16.92g; Fat: 0.49g; Sugar: 0.45g; Sodium: 335mg; Fiber: 0.1g

64 – Slow-Cooked Marinara Squid

Serves: 4
Cooking Time: 3 minutes.
Preparation Time: 3 minutes

Ingredients:
- 1 jar marinara sauce
- 2 cloves garlic, crushed
- ½ cup Parmesan cheese, grated
- 3 tablespoons olive oil
- 2-pounds squid, cleaned and sliced into rings

Instructions:
1) Pour in jar of marinara and the squid in Instant Pot.
2) Mix well.
3) Cover, press steam function, and adjust cook time to 3 minutes.
4) To serve, transfer evenly to plates and drizzle top with parmesan cheese.

Nutrition information: Calories per serving: 379; Carbohydrates: 14.91g; Protein: 40.27g; Fat: 17.06g; Sugar: 3.84g; Sodium: 338mg; Fiber: 1.6g

65 – Caper-Relish Topped Poached Salmon

Serves: 4
Cooking Time: 3 minutes
Preparation Time: 10 minutes

Ingredients:

- 1 tablespoon extra-virgin olive oil
- 1 tablespoon cider vinegar
- 2 tablespoons capers, rinsed and minced
- 1 shallot, minced
- Pepper and salt to taste
- 4 6-ounce fillets of salmon
- 2 tablespoons minced fresh tarragon, stems reserved
- 2 tablespoons minced fresh parsley, stems reserved
- 1 lemon, sliced into ¼-inch thick circles

Instructions:

1) Place lemon slices on bottom of Instant Pot and scatter herb stems on top of lemon.
2) Season salmon with pepper and salt. Then, place salmon on top of lemon slices with skin side down and touching the lemons.
3) Add water to pot until it barely touches the salmon.

4) Cover, press steam function, and adjust cooking time to 3 minutes.
5) Meanwhile, make the relish by mixing in a small bowl the olive oil, vinegar, capers, shallot, tarragon, and parsley. Season with pepper and salt to taste.
6) To serve, transfer salmon to plate and top with the relish.

Nutrition information: Calories per serving: 288; Carbohydrates: 2.08g; Protein: 37.25g; Fat: 13.61g; Sugar: 0.55g; Sodium: 182mg; Fiber: 0.4g

66 – Arugula Tapenade Over Cod

Serves: 2
Cooking Time: 2 hours
Preparation Time: 20 minutes

Ingredients:
- 1-pound cod fillet
- 1 medium lemon
- 3 cups arugula
- ½ cup pitted black olives
- 2 tablespoons capers, rinsed medium garlic clove, chopped roughly
- Pepper and salt to taste

Instructions:
1) Slice the lemon into ¼-inch thick circles and layer at the bottom of Instant Pot.
2) Season cod with pepper and salt, generously.
3) Add water into Instant Pot such that it barely covers the lemon slices.
4) Place fish on top of lemon slices.
5) Cover, press steam function, and adjust cooking time to 3 minutes.
6) Meanwhile, in a blender or food processor, process the tapenade by adding the garlic, capers, olives,

and arugula. Pulse until roughly chopped and resembles a tapenade.

7) To serve, remove cod from pot and transfer to a plate. Generously top with Arugula tapenade and enjoy.

Nutrition information: Calories per serving: 216; Carbohydrates: 7.35g; Protein: 36.44g; Fat: 4.52g; Sugar: 2.4g; Sodium: 1147mg; Fiber: 2.2g

67 – Oriental Style Fish Curry

Serves: 2
Cooking Time: 25 minutes
Preparation Time: 20 minutes

Ingredients:
- 1 cup cilantro, chopped
- 1 tablespoon turmeric, or more to taste
- 1 can coconut milk, no added sugar
- 1-pound cod fillet, cut into 1-inch cubes
- 1-inch thumb ginger, sliced into 3 equal cuts
- 3 cloves garlic, chopped
- ½ of a small onion, chopped
- 2 bay leaves
- Pepper and salt to taste
- 2 tablespoons olive oil
- 1 cup water

Instructions:
1) Press sauté button on Instant Pot and heat oil.
2) Once hot, sauté garlic and sliced ginger until garlic is browned, around a minute or two.
3) Add chopped onions and sauté until wilted, around 3 minutes.
4) Add turmeric and bay leaves. Sauté for a minute.
5) Add water and bring to a simmer, around 5 minutes.

6) Add cod fillets and cook in sauté mode for 10 minutes.
7) Stir in coconut milk, season with pepper and salt to taste.
8) Cook until heated through, around 5 minutes.
9) Stir in cilantro, serve, and enjoy.

Nutrition information: Calories per serving: 590; Carbohydrates: 11.92g; Protein: 38.77g; Fat: 44.89g; Sugar: 1.03g; Sodium: 715mg; Fiber: 2.2g

68 – Braised Sea Bass in Instant Pot

Serves: 6
Cooking Time: 3 minutes
Preparation Time: 10 minutes

Ingredients:
- 6 Sea Bass fillets (around 3-pounds total)
- Pepper and salt to taste
- 3 large leeks, cleaned and sliced thinly
- 2 fennel bulbs, thinly sliced
- 1 red bell pepper, sliced thinly
- 2 tablespoons olive oil
- 1 cup water

Instructions:
1) Pour oil in Instant Pot and ensure to cover bottom with it.
2) Add leeks, fennel, and bell pepper. Season generously with pepper and salt.
3) Toss well to coat in oil. And evenly spread on bottom of pot.
4) Season fish with pepper and salt. Place fish on top of veggies.
5) Pour water, cover, press steam function, and cook for 3 minutes.

Nutrition information: Calories per serving: 311; Carbohydrates: 13.41g; Protein: 25.71g; Fat: 7.4g; Sugar: 5.57g; Sodium: 139mg; Fiber: 3.4g

69 – Shrimp Scampi on Spaghetti Squash

Serves: 4
Cooking Time: 2 hours and 30 minutes
Preparation Time: 5 minutes

Ingredients:
- 1 tablespoon ghee
- 2 ½-teaspoons lemon-garlic seasoning
- 1 small onion, chopped
- 32-ounces low-sodium broth (chicken or vegetable)
- ¾-pounds shrimp
- 1 to 3-pounds spaghetti squash

Instructions:
1) Slice spaghetti squash crosswise and in half. Scoop out the seeds and discard.
2) Then place slow cooker on HIGH settings and add broth.
3) Stir in ghee, onions, and garlic seasoning.
4) Place squash in Instant Pot with the hole side down.
5) Cook for two hours on high or until squash is soft.
6) Stir in shrimp, cover and cook for 30 minutes more.

Nutrition information: Calories per serving: 185; Carbohydrates: 18g; Protein: 20.46g; Fat: 4.22g; Sugar: 9.9g; Sodium: 1099mg; Fiber: 3.1g

70 – Easy Steamed Golden Pomfret

Serves: 2
Cooking Time: 5 minutes
Preparation Time: 10 minutes

Ingredients:
- A pinch of salt
- 1 stalk green onions, chopped
- 2-inch thumb ginger, chopped
- 2 garlic cloves, peeled, smashed, and chopped
- ½ lemon
- 1 teaspoon sesame oil
- ¼ cup soy sauce
- ¼ cup water
- 1 teaspoon pepper
- 1 medium Golden Pomfret or Pompano

Instructions:
1) Place ½ of ginger inside the head of the Pomfret as well as ½ of the garlic.
2) Rub salt and pepper on Pomfret.
3) On Instant Pot, add remaining ginger and garlic.
4) Pour in sesame oil, lemon juice, soy sauce, and water.
5) Place pompano on a steamer basket.

6) Cover, press steam button, and adjust cooking time to 5 minutes.
7) Do a quick release.
8) Transfer pompano to a serving dish.
9) Top with chopped green onions and then pour the steaming sauce on top of fish.
10) Serve and enjoy.

Nutrition information: Calories per serving: 207; Carbohydrates: 30.04g; Protein: 4.76g; Fat: 8.55g; Sugar: 16.14g; Sodium: 571mg; Fiber: 5.4g

Chapter 9 - Instant Pot, Keto Diet Vegetable Recipes

71 – Nasi Goreng Keto Approved

Serves: 2
Cooking Time: 12 minutes
Preparation Time: 20 minutes

Ingredients:
- Salt
- Pepper
- 4 eggs
- 1 tablespoon sesame oil
- 1-ounce fresh ginger
- 2 garlic cloves
- 4-ounces butter or olive oil
- 1 red/green chili pepper, sliced thinly
- ½ green bell pepper, sliced thinly
- 2-ounces scallions, sliced thinly
- ½ yellow onion, sliced thinly
- 1-pound cauliflower
- ½ lime, zested and juiced
- ½ cup mayonnaise

Instructions:

1) In a small bowl, mix mayonnaise, lime zest, and lime juice. Mix well and set aside in the fridge.
2) In food processor, process cauliflower until rice like in size.
3) Press sauté button and heat olive oil or butter.
4) Once oil is hot, add cauliflower, bell pepper, chili, scallion, and onions. sauté for 5 minutes.
5) Add garlic and ginger. Cook for a minute.
6) Add sesame oil.
7) Season with pepper and salt to taste.
8) Clear the middle of pot and crack egg. Wait for two minutes before stirring pot and mixing the egg.
9) Transfer to plates and serve with a dollop of mayonnaise.

Nutrition information: Calories per serving: 657; Carbohydrates: 25.93g; Protein: 24.8g; Fat: 52.03g; Sugar: 10.39g; Sodium: 817mg; Fiber: 6.8g

72 – Cabbage Asian Stir-Fry

Serves: 4
Cooking Time: 25 minutes
Preparation Time: 15 minutes

Ingredients:

- 1 tablespoon sesame oil
- 1 tablespoon fresh ginger, chopped into 3 pieces
- 1 teaspoon chili flakes
- 3 scallions
- 2 garlic cloves, peeled, smashed and chopped
- 1 tablespoon white wine vinegar
- ¼ teaspoon ground black pepper
- 1 teaspoon onion powder
- 1 teaspoon salt
- 1 1/3-pounds ground beef
- 1/3-pound butter
- 1 2/3-pounds green cabbage

Instructions:

1) In food processor, shred cabbage until fine.
2) Press sauté button on Instant Pot and heat ¼ of the butter.
3) Once butter is melted, stir fry cabbage for 5 minutes or until lightly browned but not soft.

4) Mix in white vinegar, black pepper, onion powder, and salt. Sauté for two minutes and transfer to a bowl.
5) Heat remaining butter and sauté fresh ginger, chili flakes, and garlic cloves.
6) Saute for 2 minutes and add ground meat.
7) Saute until meat is browned, around 8 to 10 minutes.
8) Add cabbage back into pot.
9) Stir in scallions and mix well.
10) Taste and adjust seasoning if needed.
11) Drizzle with sesame oil, mix, and remove from pot.

Nutrition information: Calories per serving: 768; Carbohydrates: 12.66g; Protein: 41.23g; Fat: 61.89g; Sugar: 5.52g; Sodium: 1468mg; Fiber: 4.1g

73 – Brussel Sprouts with Bacon

Serves: 4
Cooking Time: 15 minutes
Preparation Time: 10 minutes

Ingredients:
- Habanero sea salt
- 1 tablespoon honey
- ½ cup water
- 3-4 slices of bacon chopped into 1-inch squares
- 4 cups chopped Brussel sprouts

Instructions:
1) Press sauté button on Instant Pot and add bacon.
2) Cook for 7 minutes, while stirring occasionally.
3) Add Brussel sprouts and cook for 5 minutes, stirring occasionally.
4) Add water and deglaze pot.
5) Cover, press cancel, press manual button, adjust pressure to high, and cooking time to 2 minutes.
6) Do a quick release.
7) Transfer vegetables in bowl, season with salt, and drizzle with honey.
8) Toss well to coat before serving.

Nutrition information: Calories per serving: 146; Carbohydrates: 12.39g; Protein: 5.84g; Fat: 9.2g; Sugar: 6.44g; Sodium: 168mg; Fiber: 3.4g

74 – Red Coconut Curry Vegetarian

Serves: 2
Cooking Time: 30 minutes
Preparation Time: 10 minutes

Ingredients:
- ½ cup coconut cream
- 1 tablespoon red curry paste
- 2 teaspoons soy sauce
- 2 teaspoons fish sauce
- 1 teaspoon minced ginger
- 1 teaspoon minced garlic
- ¼ medium onion, chopped
- 4 tablespoons coconut oil
- 1 large handful of spinach
- 1 cup broccoli

Instructions:
1) Press sauté button on Instant Pot and heat 2 tablespoons of coconut oil.
2) Sauté onions until translucent around 5 to 8 minutes.
3) Add garlic and continue to sauté until browned around 2 minutes.
4) Add broccoli and stir fry until broccoli is partially cooked around 4 minutes.

5) Clear the middle of the pot and add curry paste. Cook for a minute and then mix with the broccoli.
6) Add spinach on top of broccoli and let it wilt, around 4 minutes.
7) Stir in coconut oil and coconut cream.
8) Add ginger, fish sauce, and soy sauce. Mix well.
9) Bring to a simmer and cook for 8 minutes.

Nutrition information: Calories per serving: 380; Carbohydrates: 23.41g; Protein: 8.26g; Fat: 31.03g; Sugar: 2.62g; Sodium: 787mg; Fiber: 5.9g

75 – Stir Fry Tempeh, Spinach, Broccoli and Olives

Serves: 1
Cooking Time: 7 minutes
Preparation Time: 5 minutes

Ingredients:
- 1 tablespoon olive oil
- Pepper and salt to taste
- A dash of garlic powder
- 3-ounces tempeh
- 1 cup frozen spinach, thawed and excess liquid squeezed out
- 1 cup broccoli florets

Instructions:
1) Press sauté button and heat oil.
2) Add broccoli florets and tempeh.
3) Season with garlic powder, salt, and pepper.
4) Stir fry for 5 minutes.
5) Stir in spinach and cook until heated through, around 2 minutes.
6) Transfer to a plate, serve and enjoy.

Nutrition information: Calories per serving: 366; Carbohydrates: 22.21g; Protein: 24.12g; Fat: 23.89g; Sugar: 3.54g; Sodium: 142mg; Fiber: 6.6g

Chapter 10 –Instant Pot, Keto Vegan-Friendly Recipes

76 – Keto Fries with Peppers and Caramelized Cauliflower

Serves: 2
Cooking Time: 25 minutes
Preparation Time: 5 minutes

Ingredients:
- Salt
- Pepper
- 1 big pinch of dried dill
- ¼ teaspoon poultry seasoning
- ¼ yellow pepper
- ¼ green pepper
- ¼ red pepper
- ½ yellow onion
- 1 head cauliflower, chopped
- 1 tablespoon olive oil

Instructions:
1) Press sauté button on Instant Pot and heat oil.
2) Meanwhile, place chopped cauliflower in microwave safe bowl and add ½-inch of water. Stick into the

microwave and cook for 4 minutes. Once it is done cooking, let it sit in microwave for 2 more minutes.

3) Once oil is hot, stir fry onions and peppers and cook for a minute.
4) Add 2 tablespoons of water to veggies and continue sautéing until water is reduced.
5) Mix in dill and poultry seasoning. Sauté for a minute.
6) Strain cauliflower and dump into pot.
7) Mix in pepper and salt to taste.
8) Sauté for 5 minutes more.

Nutrition information: Calories per serving: 198; Carbohydrates: 13.95g; Protein: 6.47g; Fat: 14.15g; Sugar: 5.32g; Sodium: 132mg; Fiber: 3.8g

77 – Cauliflower Rice

Serves: 4
Cooking Time: 10 minutes
Preparation Time: 5 minutes

Ingredients:
- 3 ¼-ounces butter or coconut oil
- ½ teaspoon turmeric (optional)
- ½ teaspoon salt
- 1 2/3-pounds cauliflower

Instructions:
1) In food processor, process cauliflower until shredded and is rice like in appearance.
2) On Instant Pot, press sauté button and melt butter.
3) Once melted, stir in shredded cauliflower and cook for 8 minutes.
4) Stir in turmeric and salt. Sauté for a minute more.
5) Transfer to a plate and serve.

Nutrition information: Calories per serving: 214; Carbohydrates: 9.68g; Protein: 3.87g; Fat: 19.22g; Sugar: 3.64g; Sodium: 496mg; Fiber: 3.9g

78 – Keto-Approved Steamed Artichoke

Serves: 4
Cooking Time: 10 minutes
Preparation Time: 15 minutes

Ingredients:
- 1 pinch paprika
- 1 teaspoon Dijon mustard
- 2 tablespoons mayonnaise
- 1 lemon
- 2 medium artichokes

Instructions:
1) Wash and trim artichokes. Cut off the top edge if spiny and even surrounding leaves, cut the spines off.
2) Rub lemon on any cut edges of artichoke.
3) On Instant Pot, add a cup of water and put in steamer basket.
4) Place artichoke inside steamer basket.
5) Cover and press steam button.
6) Allow for a natural release.
7) Serve and enjoy.

Nutrition information: Calories per serving: 67; Carbohydrates: 9.95g; Protein: 3.27g; Fat: 2.65g; Sugar: 1.24g; Sodium: 148mg; Fiber: 4.7g

79 – Vegetarian Soy Curls with Butter Chicken

Serves: 6
Cooking Time: 6 minutes
Preparation Time: 15 minutes

Ingredients:
- 1 cup water
- 1 ½ cups dry soy curls
- 1 teaspoon cumin powder
- 1 teaspoon garam masala
- 1 teaspoon salt
- 1 teaspoon paprika
- ½ teaspoon cayenne pepper
- 1 teaspoon turmeric
- 1-2 teaspoon ginger minced
- 5-6 cloves garlic minced
- 1 14-ounce can diced tomatoes
- 4-ounce heavy cream
- ¼ cup chopped cilantro

Instructions:
1) On Instant Pot, add water, dry soy curls, cumin powder, garam masala, salt, paprika, cayenne pepper, turmeric, ginger, garlic, and tomatoes.
2) Mix well.

3) Cover, press manual button, choose high pressure, and adjust cook time to 6 minutes.
4) Then for 10 minutes, allow Instant Pot to do a natural release and then release pressure manually after that.
5) Mix in heavy cream and mix well.
6) Transfer to a serving bowl and garnish tops with cilantro.

Nutrition information: Calories per serving: 76; Carbohydrates: 7.66g; Protein: 6.66g; Fat: 4.55g; Sugar: 2.12g; Sodium: 2760mg; Fiber: 2.1g

80 – Brussels Sprouts, Spinach and Hummus

Serves: 1
Cooking Time: 10 minutes
Preparation Time: 10 minutes

Ingredients:
- 1 teaspoon garlic powder
- 1 tablespoon olive oil
- Pepper and salt to taste
- 4 tablespoons hummus
- 1 cup frozen spinach, thawed and excess liquid squeezed out
- 1 cup Brussels sprouts, halved

Instructions:
1) Press sauté button.
2) Heat oil and once hot sauté Brussels sprouts, for 5 minutes.
3) Season with garlic powder, pepper, and salt.
4) Stir in Spinach and cook until heated through around 2 minutes.
5) Transfer to a bowl and add a dollop of hummus and enjoy.

Nutrition information: Calories per serving: 319; Carbohydrates: 28.77g; Protein: 12.07g; Fat: 19.83g; Sugar: 3.19g; Sodium: 285mg; Fiber: 10.5g

Chapter 10 – Instant Pot, Keto Dessert Recipes

81 – Cream and Berries Cake with Whipped Brown Sugar

Serves: 1
Cooking Time: 10 minutes
Preparation Time: 15 minutes

Ingredients:
- ¼ cup mixed berries
- ¼ cup almond flour
- 2 tablespoons organic cream cheese
- 2 tablespoons ghee
- ¼ cup sugar-free vanilla bean sweetener syrup
- 2 large eggs
- ¼ cup heavy whipping cream
- ½ tablespoon sugar-free brown sugar syrup

Instructions:
1) In a blender, mix cream cheese, ghee, vanilla bean sweetener, and eggs until smooth.
2) Transfer into a heat proof bowl and cover top with foil.
3) Add a cup of water in Instant Pot.

4) Add steamer basket and place bowl on top.
5) Cover and press steam button.
6) Meanwhile, whip your cream until stiff and slowly add the brown sugar syrup. Store in fridge.
7) Once done steaming, do a quick release and allow cake to cool.
8) Refrigerate for at least 2 hours, top with whipped cream, and enjoy.

Nutrition information: Calories per serving: 495; Carbohydrates: 67.7g; Protein: 9.14g; Fat: 21.15g; Sugar: 51.53g; Sodium: 258mg; Fiber: 1.1g

82 – Chocolate Salty Treat

Serves: 10
Cooking Time: 15 minutes
Preparation Time: 5 minutes

Ingredients:
- Sea salt
- 1 tablespoon pumpkin seeds
- 2 tablespoons roasted unsweetened coconut chips
- 10 hazelnuts or pecan/walnuts
- 3 ½-ounces dark chocolate (minimum of 70% cocoa solids)

Instructions:
1) On Instant Pot, add 1/2 cup of water and press sauté button.
2) On a heat proof bowl, place chocolate and slowly lower into Instant Pot.
3) Continue heating bowl until chocolate is melted. If needed you can add more water into Instant Pot.
4) Once chocolate is melted, stir in salt, pumpkin seeds, coconut chips, and walnuts.
5) Refrigerate for at least two hours, cut into strips and enjoy.

Nutrition information: Calories per serving: 83; Carbohydrates: 8.13g; Protein: 1.35g; Fat: 5.07g; Sugar: 5.14g; Sodium: 13mg; Fiber: 1g

83 – Chocolate Fudge

Serves: 24
Cooking Time: 25 minutes
Preparation Time: 20 minutes

Ingredients:
- 3 ¼-ounces dark chocolate with a minimum of 70% cocoa, chopped
- 3 ¼-ounces butter
- 1 teaspoon vanilla extract
- 2 cups heavy whipping cream

Instructions:
1) Press sauté button on Instant Pot.
2) Add vanilla and heavy cream and bring to a simmer.
3) Continue simmering for 20 minutes or until mixture is reduced to 50% its original amount. Stir frequently to prevent burning.
4) Press cancel button and stir in butter.
5) Mix well until butter is melted and thoroughly incorporated.
6) Add chocolate and mix until thoroughly melted and combined.
7) In a square baking dish, grease bottom and sides with cooking spray, pour in chocolate mixture.
8) Stick into the fridge for at least 4 hours.

9) Slice into 24 equal pieces and enjoy.
10) Refrigerate at all times.

Nutrition information: Calories per serving: 83; Carbohydrates: 2.35g; Protein: 0.58g; Fat: 8.13g; Sugar: 1.99g; Sodium: 31mg; Fiber: 0.2g

84 – Macadamia Nut Brownies

Serves: 9
Cooking Time: 10 minutes
Preparation Time: 25 minutes

Ingredients:
- 1 teaspoon instant coffee
- 1 teaspoon vanilla extract
- 1 ½ teaspoon baking powder
- 2 large eggs
- 3 tablespoon cocoa powder
- 5 tablespoon salted butter
- ¼ cup coconut oil
- ¾ cup macadamia nuts
- ¾ cup erythritol
- ¾ cup Honeyville almond flour

Instructions:
1) In a mixing bowl, cream butter.
2) Add erythritol and coconut oil and mix well.
3) Add vanilla and eggs, mix for around a minute or until fully incorporated.
4) Add coffee and cocoa powder and mix well.
5) Add almond flour and baking powder and mix thoroughly.
6) With a spatula, fold in macadamia nuts.

7) Transfer batter to a heat proof dish that fits inside your Instant Pot.
8) Spread evenly and cover top with foil.
9) On Instant Pot, add a cup of water and steamer basket.
10) Place dish of batter in side steamer basket.
11) Cover, press steam button.
12) Allow for natural release, slice into 9 equal servings, and enjoy.

Nutrition information: Calories per serving: 189; Carbohydrates: 3.29g; Protein: 1.89g; Fat: 20.04g; Sugar: 0.63g; Sodium: 38mg; Fiber: 1.5g

85 – Mocha Pudding Cake

Serves: 6
Cooking Time: 2 hours 10 minutes
Preparation Time: 25 minutes

Ingredients:
- 2/3 cup granulated sweetener
- 5 large eggs
- 1/8 teaspoon salt
- 1/3 cup almond flour
- 4 tablespoons unsweetened cocoa powder
- 1 teaspoon vanilla extract
- 2 tablespoons instant coffee crystals
- ½ cup heavy cream
- 2-ounces unsweetened chocolate
- ¾ cup butter
- Coconut oil spray

Instructions:
1) Grease sides and bottom of Instant Pot with cooking spray.
2) Press sauté button.
3) Add butter and chocolate. Mix well. Make sure to mix constantly so as the bottom doesn't burn. Once fully incorporated, press cancel to keep warm.

4) Meanwhile, in a small bowl whisk well vanilla, coffee crystals, and heavy cream.
5) In another bowl, mix well salt, almond flour, and cocoa powder.
6) In a mixing bowl, beat eggs until thick and pale, around 5 minutes while slowly stirring in sweetener.
7) While beating, slowly drizzle and mix in melted butter mixture.
8) Mix in the almond flour mixture and mix well.
9) Add the coffee mixture and beat until fully incorporated.
10) Pour batter into Instant Pot.
11) Place a paper towel on top of pot this will absorb condensation.
12) Cover pot, press slow cooker button, and adjust to 2-hour cooking time.

Nutrition information: Calories per serving: 397; Carbohydrates: 27.92g; Protein: 3.59g; Fat: 31.21g; Sugar: 21.93g; Sodium: 253mg; Fiber: 1.4g

Made in the USA
San Bernardino, CA
09 September 2017